JAIIB

Accounting & Finance for Bankers

Latest Edition
Practice Kit

05 Tests
05 Mock Test

Based On Real Exam Pattern

✓ Thoroughly Revised and Updated

✓ Detailed Analysis of all MCQs

Title	: JAIIB Accounting & Finance for Bankers
Author Name	: Mr. Rohit Manglik
Published By	: EduGorilla Community Pvt. Ltd.
Publishers Address	: 12/651, First Floor Opp. Arvindo Park, Near Jama Masjid, Indira Nagar, Lucknow, Uttar Pradesh-226016, India

Copyright EduGorilla

Disclaimer EduGorilla

Compiled and created by EduGorilla Community Pvt. Ltd

Printed By EduGorilla Community Pvt. Ltd.

ROHIT MANGLIK
CEO, EduGorilla

Dear Applicants,

People say *"Success comes to those who work hard."* But I've seen people working hard for their exams day in and day out for marginal success. While others succeed in their examinations by putting in just half the work. So are they God Gifted? No! I believe that it's because they work *smart* and not just *hard*. Similarly, for your exams, you should strategize your preparation so as to increase the likelihood of success. Well with EduGorilla get ready to increase your *chances of selection* in your exam by *16x*.

EduGorilla helps you in not only working *hard* but also working in a *smart and strategic* manner. With EduGorilla's preparation package, you get a chance to make your exam preparation easy, and a fun learning path towards selection. Finding the right path to your preparations can be difficult if you don't know in which direction to head. Don't worry, we have you covered! EduGorilla will be your guide to success in your journey. With our Preparation Package, you can prepare strategically and beat the exam in just one attempt.

EduGorilla's Preparation Package includes-

- **Test Series**
- **Books**

Our preparation package is handcrafted as per the latest changes, expert opinions, and students' discretion. Thus, enabling you to get through each stage of the selection process for your exam.

Our Books are designed by the teachers and experts of the respective exam with a combined 150+ years of experience; to provide you with easy, efficient, and effective learning. Our books are smart, in the sense that not only do they give you the answers to the questions but also provide similar questions for practice.

EduGorilla's competent Test Series gives you real-time experience and confidence through which you can clear your offline or online exam in just one attempt. We currently host 83,000+ mock tests for 1,440+ competitive and academic exams.

Thus, EduGorilla misses no chance to assist you in your preparation and covers all stages of the exam, so that you don't have to look anywhere else.

We provide complete preparation packages for defense, banking, teaching, and other National & State-Level exams. Hence, it doesn't matter which exam you aspire to because you will reach your success.

ALL THE BEST !
Let EduGorilla be your Guide to Success.

Rohit Manglik,
Founder and CEO, EduGorilla

INTRODUCTION

EduGorilla focuses on guiding students to succeed in their examinations. With that in mind, our book, titled "JAIIB : Accounting & Finance for Bankers", has been drafted through the collective efforts of our distinguished experts with 150+ years of combined experience. This book consists of questions that are created following the latest changes in the syllabus and exam pattern. We compiled the book on the basis of questions that are most likely to appear in the JAIIB Exam. Through EduGorilla's "JAIIB : Accounting & Finance for Bankers" your chances of success will increase 16x.

EduGorilla does this through our Complete Preparation Package. This package consists of well-conceptualized and structured content in the form of questions that are tailor-made according to your needs and will help you practice for exams in a smart way by pinpointing all the necessary information. It also provides hints and solutions, along with a smart answer sheet for your self-evaluation. You can assess your shortcomings and work accordingly on areas that may require more of your attention.

EduGorilla promises to help you succeed in your examination and accomplish your dream goals. We believe in our aspirants and see them at the top of the merit list. And the first step towards the top is to start preparing with us. EduGorilla's "JAIIB : Accounting & Finance for Bankers" includes the following attributes.

➤ Well-Researched Content

➤ Top-Notch Quality

➤ Detailed Answers and Analysis

➤ Smart Answer Sheet

➤ Exam Relevant Questions

Therefore, EduGorilla fortifies your preparation and makes it durable enough to help you stand tall and beat the examination.

JAIIB Exam
Scan QR code for Eligibility, Exam Pattern, Syllabus and more.

Book ID: 0707

TABLE OF CONTENTS

Mock Test 01

Q.1 E-commerce means:

A. electronic commerce.

B. buying and selling on the web.

C. a way of enabling business over the net.

D. All of the above

Q.2 In real online banking

A. transactions are entered through the terminal and recorded immediately, but updations are done later on.

B. transactions are entered through the terminal and recorded immediately, but authentication, verification, and updations are done later on.

C. transactions are entered through the terminal and then they are recorded, verified, authenticated, and corresponding updations are reflected instantly.

D. None of the above

Q.3 For a computerized accounting system, the system means

A. software programs.

B. computer peripherals.

C. data.

D. Both (A) and (B)

Q.4 The instructions fed to the computer to process data are known as

A. softwares.

B. hardware.

C. programs.

D. information.

Q.5 The twentieth century has been the century of the advent of

A. internet.

B. e-mail.

C. e-commerce.

D. All of the above

Q.6 Which of the following capital is taken up by the general public?

A. Issued capital

B. Subscribed capital

C. Authorized capital

D. Reserve capital

Q.7 Under ________ majority of transactions are processed online.

A. transaction processing

B. online processing

C. multiprocessing

D. None of the above

Q.8 CRM stands for:

A. Consumer Relationship Management.

B. Customer Relationship Management.

C. Care Relationship Management.

D. Cube Relationship Management.

Q.9 ______ is one of the main issues that banks face in today's hyper-competitive environment.

A. Managing customers

B. Cut costs

C. Manage competition

D. All of the above

Q.10 Technique which enables the company to select the best alternative from among a number of alternative proposals is called

A. finance plan.

B. marginal costing.

C. capital budgeting.

D. capital structure.

Q.11 From the following details:

Particulars	Rs.
Opening Debtors	10,200
Cash received from debtors	30,400
Return Inwards	2,700
Bad debts	1,200
Debtors at end	13,800
Cash Sales	28,400

Find out the total sales?

A. Rs.66,300

B. Rs.66,000

C. Rs.65,000

D. Rs.66,500

Q.12 A cheque returned by bank marked "NSF" means that

A. the bank can't verify your identity.

B. there are not sufficient funds in your account.

C. the cheque has been forged.

D. cheque can't be cashed being illegal.

Q.13 On 31st March 2011, the books Ajit showed a net profit of Rs. 84,000. Later it was discovered that the closing stock was overvalued by 4,000 and the discount received of Rs. 1,500 was treated as an expense. What was the correct net profit of Ajit?

A. Rs. 81,500

B. Rs. 83,000

C. Rs. 89,500

D. Rs. 91,000

Q.14 While taking stock for the purpose of preparation of trading account, stock in hand on the last day of the accounting year should be adjusted for purchases recorded but goods not received, goods sold but not yet delivered and goods that may be out of business premises because of consignment, goods delivered on sale or return basis, and so on.

A. True

B. False because stock in hand at the beginning day of the accounting year should be adjusted

C. False because no adjustment is required for goods delivered on sale or return basis

D. False because of both (B) and (C)

Q.15 P sold goods to Q for Rs. 2,00,000. Q paid cash Rs. 60,000. P allowed a discount of 2% on the balance. What is the amount of the bill drawn by P on Q?

A. Rs. 1,96,000

B. Rs. 1,37,200

C. Rs. 1,40,000

D. Rs. 1,36,000

Q.16 Which of the following entries is correct in respect of reserve for discounts on accounts payable?

(a) Profit & Loss A/c	To Reserve for Discount on Accounts Payable A/c Dr.
(b) Accounts Payable A/c	To Profit& Loss A/c Dr.
(c) Reserve for Discount on Accounts Payable A/c	To Profit & Loss A/c Dr.
(d) Reserve for Discount on Accounts Payable A/c	To Accounts Payable A/c Dr.

A. (a)   **B.** (b)   **C.** (c)   **D.** (d)

Q.17 Even when two projects are mutually exclusive, capital rationing results in the accurate ranking by

A. NPV method only.

B. IRR method only.

C. NPV as well as IRR method.

D. None of the above

Q.18 Depreciable assets are assets which

A. are expected to be used during more than one accounting period.

B. have a limited useful life.

C. are held by an enterprise for use in the production for supply of goods and services, for rental to others, or to administrative purposes and not for the purpose of sale in the ordinary course of business.

D. All of the above

Q.19 What is the formula for the Accounting Rate of Return?

A. Average Profit after Tax + Average Book Value of Investment.

B. Average Profit after Tax – Average Book Value of Investment.

C. Average Profit after Tax × Average Book Value of Investment.

D. Average Profit after Tax ÷ Average Book Value of Investment.

Q.20 _______ decisions require evaluation of proposals to diversify into new product lines, new markets etc.

A. Replacement and modernization

B. Expansion

C. Diversification

D. Mutually exclusive

Q.21 Consider a bond that offers a 10% p.a. rate of interest to be compounded half-yearly. What is the effective rate of interest per annum?

A. 10%   **B.** 10.25%   **C.** 5%   **D.** 20%

Q.22 RTGS stands for:

A. Real-Time Gross Settlement.

B. Reel Time Gross Settlement.

C. Real Type Gross Settlement.

D. None of the above

Q.23 When preparing Bank Reconciliation Statement, if you start with balance as per Pass Book, then cheques paid by bank recorded twice in Pass Book as Rs.1,050 will be _________.

A. added

B. deducted

C. not required to be adjusted

D. None of the above

Q.24 An entry has been made in the credit column of a bank statement but not recorded in the cash book. Such record can be

A. bank charges.   **B.** direct payment.

C. credit transfer.   **D.** represented cheque.

Q.25 The bank balance shown in the balance sheet of an organization is

A. balance as per passbook.

B. higher than the balance as per passbook.

C. corrected balance as per passbook.

D. corrected balance as per cash book.

Q.26 In the case of dishonor of cheque/bill receivable, the amount is recorded in the cash book

A. after the entry is posted in the pass book.

B. when the cheque is dishonoured.

C. when the amount is paid by the bank.

D. when the amount is collected by the bank.

Q.27 _______ is a copy of the clients' account in the bank's ledger.

A. Passbook   **B.** Cash book

C. Cheque book   **D.** Trial balance

Q.28 The client can instruct the bank to collect money, say interest or dividend on investments made by the client and to make payments say premiums of insurance policy on his behalf. The bank ______ the client's account with such collections made and _______ the clients account with such payments.

A. credits, credits   **B.** debits, debits

C. credits, debits   **D.** debits, credits

Q.29 The difference in Bank Balance as per Pass Book and Cash Book may arise on account of

A. cheque issued but not presented.

B. cheque issued but dishonoured.

C. cheque deposited and credited by the bank.

D. Both (A) and (B)

Q.30 On 31st March 2012, bank balance as per pass book (Cr.) Rs. 20,000. A comparison of passbook and cashbook revealed the following:

- Cheques deposited for Rs. 20,000 out of these cheques bank had credited cheques of Rs. 5,000.

- Bank charges Rs. 100 was not entered in cash books.

- Balance as per cash book will be _______ .

A. Rs.40,100   **B.** Rs.35,100

C. Rs.100   **D.** Rs.4,900

Q.31 Bank reconciliation is a statement prepared to reconcile

A. trial balance.

B. cash book.

C. bank account.

D. bank balance as per cash book with a bank balance as per bank passbook.

Q.32 The implementation of KYC in banks primarily addresses which one of the following risks?

A. Reputation risk

B. Legal risk

C. Money laundering risk

D. Compliance risk

Q.33 Banks generally prefer debt equity ratio at_________.

A. 1 : 1   **B.** 1 : 3   **C.** 2 : 1   **D.** 3 : 1

Q.34 _____ ratio expresses the relationship between what is available as earnings per share and what is actually paid in the form of dividends out of available earnings.

A. Price earning   **B.** Payout

C. Dividend yield   **D.** Debt. equity

Q.35 Proprietary Ratio = $\dfrac{Shareholder's\ Funds}{?}$

A. Long Term Funds   **B.** Fixed Assets

C. Total Assets   **D.** Interest Charges

Q.36 Debtor collection period depends upon the

A. nature of the industry.

B. seasonal character of the business.

C. credit policy of the firm.

D. All of the above

Q.37 The ratio of all operating expenses (i.e. materials used, labour, factory overheads, office and selling expenses) to sales is the ______ ratio.

A. gross Profit   **B.** net Profit

C. operating   **D.** activity

Q.38 Capital employed = ?

A. Net Fixed Assets + Working Capital

B. Net Fixed Assets – Working Capital

C. Net Fixed Assets ×Working Capital

D. Net Fixed Assets ÷ Working Capital

Q.39 A measure of profitability is the overall measure of efficiency.

A. True   **B.** False

C. Partly true   **D.** Partly false

Q.40 The ratio used by bankers to ascertain the long term solvency of a business is

A. debt. equity ratio.

B. current ratio.

C. debtor turnover ratio.

D. net profit ratio.

Q.41 Ratios act as indicators of

A. Financial soundness   **B.** Strength

C. Position   **D.** All of the above

Q.42 The term _________ means manipulation of accounts in such a way as to conceal vital facts and present the financial statements in such a way as to show a better position than what actually is.

A. window dressing   **B.** short term solvency

C. long term solvency   **D.** profitability

Q.43 To make provision for bad debts, which of the following journal entries is correct?

A. Debit. the profit and loss, and credit the bad debt account

B. Debit. the profit and loss account, and credit provision on the bad debt account

C. Debit. the provision account and credit the bad debt account

D. Debit. the provision and credit the account of the individual customers

Q.44 A machine was purchased two years ago for Rs. 2,00,000. It is depreciated at the rate of 20% p.a. by the straight-line method and presently, its market value is Rs. 1,00,000. According to the cost concept, it should be recorded in the books at

A. Rs. 2,00,000   **B.** Rs. 1,00,000

C. Rs. 1,20,000   **D.** Rs. 1,60,000

Q.45 Right shares are issued to

A. promoters for the services.

B. holders of convertible debentures.

C. existing shareholders.

D. All of the above

Q.46 The shares should be issued in

A. lots as decided by FEMA.

B. tradable lot.

C. fractional lot.

D. odd lot.

Q.47 When the shares are not payable in a lump sum, they can be called in a number of installments. Here, the first installment is called the

A. application money.   **B.** allotment money.

C. first, call money.   **D.** final call money.

Q.48 The prescribed form of the Balance Sheet requires that under the head Issued Capital, ______ should be stated.

A. the different classes of share capital

B. the sub-classes of preference shares

C. Either (A) or (B)

D. None of the above

Q.49 A and B invest in a business in the ratio 3:2. If 5% of the total profit goes to charity and A's share is Rs. 855, the total profit is-

A. Rs.1425   **B.** Rs.1500

C. Rs.1537.50   **D.** Rs.1576

Q.50 According to the Companies Act, 2013, the Balance Sheet is prepared as per

A. Part II Schedule VI.

B. Part I Schedule III.

C. Part II Schedule VII.

D. Part I Schedule VII.

Q.51 X Ltd. acquired assets worth Rs. 7,50,000 from Y Ltd. by the issue of shares of Rs. 100 at a premium of 25%. The number

of shares to be issued by X Ltd. to settle the purchase consideration will be

A. 6,000 shares.
B. 7,500 shares.
C. 9,375 shares.
D. 5,625 shares.

Q.52 The companies which are formed under the Special Act are called

A. chartered companies.
B. statutory companies.
C. registered companies.
D. None of these

Q.53 The expansion of CAPM is __________.

A. the capital amount pricing model
B. the capital asset pricing model
C. the capital asset printing model
D. the capital amount printing model

Q.54 The minimum number of Directors in the case of a public company is

A. 1   **B.** 2   **C.** 3   **D.** 4

Q.55 The building's account is debited with an amount towards repairs. This is an example of

A. the error of omission.
B. the error of principle.
C. the error of commission.
D. the error of compensation.

Q.56 Rs. 4,500 is paid to Rohan as salary for the month of December 2012, which was debited from his account. This is an error of ____.

A. principle
B. omission
C. commission
D. compensation

Q.57 A suspense account is a __________.

A. temporary account
B. permanent account
C. loan account
D. liability account

Q.58 A trial balance contains the balances of

A. personal account and real account.
B. real account and nominal account.
C. nominal account and personal account.
D. real account, personal account, and nominal account.

Q.59 Trial balance is a/an

A. statement.
B. account.
C. summary.
D. ledger.

Q.60 Closing stock in the Trial Balance implies that

A. it is already adjusted in the Opening Stock.
B. it is adjusted in the Purchase Account.
C. it is adjusted in the Cost of Sale Account.
D. it is adjusted in the Profit and Loss Account.

Q.61 Net working capital is the excess of current asset over __________.

A. current liability
B. net liability
C. total payable
D. total liability

Q.62 Short term sources are

A. bank credit.
B. public deposit.
C. commercial papers.
D. All of the above

Q.63 Rs. 2,500 spent on the overhauling on purchase of second hand machinery is

A. capital expenditure.
B. revenue expenditure.
C. deferred revenue expenditure.
D. None of the above

Q.64 For mutual accommodation, A accepted a bill of 2 months for Rs. 10,000 drawn on him by B. B discounted the bill at 12% p.a. Out of the proceeds, A receives

A. Rs. 9,800
B. Rs. 8,100
C. Rs. 4,900
D. Rs. 5,000

Q.65 The bill of Rs. 10,000 accepted by Mr. P on 1 July 2009 was discounted by Mr. R on 15 July 2009 for Rs. 9,600. On 4 October 2009, the bill was dishonored and the bank paid noting charges of Rs. 200 for it. The amount to be received from Mr. P would be

A. Rs. 10,600
B. Rs. 10,000
C. Rs. 10,200
D. Rs. 10,400

Q.66 The arbitrary process is the behavioral foundation for the __________.

A. MM approach
B. XX approach
C. gorder approach
D. miller approach

Q.67 Endorsement of the bill means

A. transfer of right on the bill from the drawee to the creditors.
B. transfer of right on the bill from the creditors to the drawee.
C. transfer of right on the bill from the drawer to the creditors.
D. transfer of right on the bill from the creditors to the drawer.

Q.68 Operating leverage x financial leverage = ____.

A. combined Leverage
B. financial Combined Leverage
C. operating Combined Leverage
D. fixed leverage

Q.69 ____ is the date on which a bill falls due for payment.

A. Settlement date
B. Maturity date
C. Payment date
D. Due date

Q.70 Bills payable discounted in cash by creditor will be shown in

A. journal
B. ledger
C. bank book
D. No entry required

Q.71 How many parties are generally found in a Bill of Exchange?

A. 4   **B.** 2   **C.** 3   **D.** 5

Q.72 The company's cost of capital is called _______.

A. leverage
B. hurdle rate

C. risk rate   **D.** return rate

Q.73 Ram and Mohan are partners in a business. Their capitals at the end of the year were Rs. 24,000 and Rs. 18,000 respectively. During the year, Ram's drawings and Mohan's drawings were Rs. 4,000 and Rs. 6,000 respectively. Profit (before charging interest on capital) during the year was Rs. 16,000. Calculate interest on capital @ 5% p.a. for the year ended 31st March, 2018.

A. 1000, 900   **B.** 1080, 800
C. 1000, 800   **D.** 1000, 645

Q.74 Given information:

Capital at the end= Rs.7,000

Capital introduced = Rs.5,000

Drawings= Rs.8,000

Loss= Rs.10,000

With the above information, capital in the beginning is equal to __________.

A. $Rs.\,12,000$ **B.** $Rs.\,16,000$
C. $Rs.\,20,000$ **D.** $Rs.\,30,000$

Q.75 The amount which, as a result of operations, is added to the capital is called

A. revenue.
B. net profit.
C. drawings.
D. sales cost of goods sold.

Q.76 _________ concept requires that assets and profits not be over-stated.

A. Going Concerned   **B.** Prudence
C. Duality   **D.** Accounting Period

Q.77 Which of the following statements is true?

A. Going concern concept assumes that business will be carried on for a definite period.
B. The capital losses need not be deducted to ascertain net income.
C. Provision for bad and doubtful debts is created according to the concept of conservatism.
D. The materiality concept states that all business transactions are to be recorded however insignificant they may be.

Q.78 Expenses and earnings should not be based on different years. Which concept states this?

A. Conservatism Concept
B. Consistency Concept
C. Matching Concept
D. Realization Concept

Q.79 Savings accounts are_________ but are not________.

A. negotiable, liquid   **B.** marketable, liquid
C. liquid, personal   **D.** liquid, marketable

Q.80 Recording of capital contributed by the owner as liability ensures the adherence to the principle of

A. double Entry.   **B.** going Concerned.
C. separate Entity.   **D.** materiality.

Q.81 Nominal accounts are related to

A. expenses, losses, and incomes
B. debtors and creditors
C. assets and liabilities
D. contingent liabilities

Q.82 The three columns on each side of the three columnar cash book represents

A. Real accounts
B. Nominal accounts
C. Nominal and personal accounts
D. Real, personal and nominal accounts

Q.83 Which of the following statements is/are true?

(i) Drawing account is a nominal account.

(ii) Capital account is a real account.

(iii) Sales account is a nominal account.

(iv) Outstanding salaries account is a nominal account.

(v) Patents account is a personal account.

A. Only (i)   **B.** Only (iii)
C. Both (ii) and (iv)   **D.** (ii), (iv) and (v)

Q.84 A journal is also known as

A. memorandum account.
B. kaccha book.
C. book of original entry.
D. proper book.

Q.85 A ledger contains various ___________ in it.

A. transactions   **B.** entries
C. accounts   **D.** None of these

Q.86 Rent due for the month of March is recorded ______ in the cash book.

A. on receipts side   **B.** on payments side
C. as contra   **D.** nowhere

Q.87 Cashbook records

A. only cash sales.
B. all types of cash receipts and payments.
C. only revenue receipts.
D. only capital receipts.

Q.88 If the Petty Cash fund is not reimbursed just prior to year-end and an appropriate adjusting entry is not made, then

A. the petty cash account is to be returned to the company's cashier.
B. expenses are overstated and cash is understated.
C. cash is overstated and expenses are understated.
D. cash is overstated and expenses are overstated.

Q.89 ______ implies speeding up collection on receivables, if the foreign currency in which they are invoiced, is expected to appreciate.

A. Leading   **B.** Lagging
C. Netting   **D.** Matching

Q.90 The exchange rate between two currencies calculated on the basis of the rate of these two currencies in terms of a third currency is known as

A. direct quote

B. indirect quote

C. cross rate

D. forward rate

Q.91 In the spot exchange market, the quote may be denoted as

A. direct.

B. indirect.

C. Both (A) and (B)

D. None of the above

Q.92 Foreign Exchange Market is also referred to as

A. inter-bank.

B. over the counter (OTC).

C. Both (A) and (B)

D. None of the above

Q.93 AS 7 deals with accounting for

A. construction contracts.

B. research and development.

C. government grants.

D. investments.

Q.94 AS 28 should be applied in accounting for impairment of all assets, except

A. inventories (AS 2) and assets arising under construction contracts (AS 7).

B. financial assets including investment covered under AS 13 and deferred tax assets (AS 22).

C. Both (A) and (B)

D. financial assets.

Q.95 AS 11 requires the enterprise to disclose

A. the number of exchange differences including the net profit or loss for the period.

B. the number of exchange differences adjusted in the carrying amount of fixed assets.

C. the number of exchange differences in respect of forwarding exchange contracts to be recognized in the profit or loss in one or more subsequent accounting period (over the life of the contract).

D. All of the above

Q.96 _______ deals with the treatment and disclosure requirements in the financial statements of events occurring after the balance sheet.

A. AS 4

B. AS 5

C. AS 6

D. AS 7

Q.97 Accounting Standards (ASs) provide

A. framework

B. standard accounting policies

C. Both (A) and (B)

D. None of the above

Q.98 The disadvantage of accounting standards is that they

A. facilitate the comparison of non-comparable accounts.

B. set the trend towards rigidity and eliminate flexibility.

C. override the law of the land.

D. None of the above

Q.99 Accounting Standards Board (ASB) was constituted by

A. ICAI

B. ICSI

C. ICWAI

D. SEBI

Q.100 Accounting standards are written policy documents issued by

A. SEBI.

B. body of Individuals.

C. FEMA.

D. expert accounting body.

Q.101 "The process of identifying, measuring and communicating economic information to permit informed judgments and decisions by the users of accounts" has been given by

A. American Institute of Certified Public Accountants (AICPA).

B. American Accounting Association.

C. Prof R. J. Chambers.

D. Kohler.

Q.102 Abhishek has two receivers. Rs.15,000 every year for 15 years. Calculate the present value of annuity assuming interest rate to be 8% p.a. (Calculation from present value to be taken up to four decimal places).

A. Rs. 1,25,000

B. Rs. 1,25,392

C. Rs. 2,25,000

D. Rs. 1,28,288

Q.103 When a company uses debt fund in its financial structure, it will lead to a change in

A. financial leverage

B. operating leverage

C. money market leverage

D. stock market leverage

Q.104 Sania deposited Rs. 50,000 in a bank for two years with the interest rate of 5.5% p.a. What will be the final value of investment?

A. Rs. 50,000

B. Rs. 50,500

C. Rs. 55,500

D. Rs. 55,000

Q.105 The banking business mainly consists of

A. lending.

B. borrowing.

C. purchasing.

D. securing.

Q.106 An advance giving income on continuous basis is called

A. performing asset.

B. non-performing asset.

C. income recognition.

D. None of the above

Q.107 Under the head Operating Expenses, printing and stationery include

A. books, forms and stationery used by the bank.

B. other printing charges which are not incurred by way of public expenditure.

C. Both (A) and (B)

D. None of the above

Q.108 ______ contains the total accounts of each ledger.

A. General ledger

B. Profit and Loss ledger

C. Personal ledger

D. Bills register

Q.109 A cash discount is

(i) the allowance to expedite cash receipts and payments within a specified period.

(ii) it is a loss for the firm receiving the payment and again for the firm making the payment.

(iii) discount allowed is entered on the debit side and discount earned on the credit side of the cash book.

A. Only (i) and (ii) **B.** Only (i) and (iii)

C. Only (ii) and (iii) **D.** (i), (ii) and (iii)

Q.110 In an account is classified as high risk, the fresh KYC documents are be obtained after________ years.

A. 10 years **B.** 8 years **C.** 3 years **D.** 2 years

Q.111 What will be the journal entry if credit sales of Rs.15400 of X Ltd. have been entered in the sales day book as Rs. 14500. Which of the following entries will correct this error?

A. Debit X Ltd. account and credit sales account with Rs. 15400

B. Debit X Ltd. account and credit sales account with Rs. 900

C. Debit sales account and credit X Ltd. account with Rs. 900

D. Debit cash account and credit sales account with Rs. 900

Q.112 Marketable securities are primarily________.

A. short-term debt instruments

B. short-term equity securities

C. long-term debt instruments

D. long-term equity securities

Q.113 Bonus share are not permitted unless the __________ shares, if any, are made fully-paid.

A. partly paid **B.** semi paid

C. fully paid **D.** unpaid

Q.114 Bill received rs. 3600, whose maturity date is after 3 months, is discounted today at the rate of 6% p.a. The correct entry is

A. Bad Debts A/c Dr 3,600
To Cash A/c 3,546
To Discount A/c 54

B. Cash A/c Dr 3,600
To B/R A/c 3,600

C. Cash A/c Dr 3546
Discount A/c Dr 54
To B/R A/c 3600

D. None of these

Q.115 Interest charged on drawings is Rs. 1,200. The correct entry is

A. Capital A/c Dr 1,200
To Interest on drawings a/c 1,200

B. Drawings A/c Dr 1,200
To Cash A/c 1,200

C. Interest on drawings A/c Dr 1,200
To Drawings A/c 1,200

D. None of these

Q.116 Bad debt of Rs. 770 is written off. The correct entry is

A. Bad debts A/c Dr 770
To debtor's A/c 770

B. Cash A/c Dr 770
To debtor's A/c 770

C. Debtors A/c Dr 770
To bad debts A/c 770

D. None of these

Q.117 The basic assumptions or conditions upon the edifice of which the accounting superstructure is based is called:

A. Accounting concepts

B. Accounting convention

C. Accounting procedure

D. Accounting standards

Q.118 Net income available to stockholders is Rs 125 and total assets are Rs 1,096 then return on common equity would be

A. 0.11% **B.** 11.40%

C. 0.12 times **D.** 12.00%

Q.119 Profit margin = 4.5%, assets turnover = 2.2 times, equity multiplier = 2.7 times then return on equity will be

A. 26.73% **B.** 25.73% **C.** 9.40% **D.** 9.00%

Q.120 When drawings are made by a partner on the last day of every month, interest should be charged from him for ___ months.

A. 5.5 **B.** 6 **C.** 6.5 **D.** 12

// Smart Answer Sheet //

Correct — Indicates percentage of students who answered questions correctly.

Skipped — Indicates percentage of students who skipped questions.

Q.	Ans.	Correct / Skipped
1	D	66.76 % / 17.05 %
2	C	56.34 % / 28.41 %
3	D	53.22 % / 25.28 %
4	C	42.61 % / 31.16 %
5	D	54.83 % / 30.68 %
6	A	31.06 % / 28.41 %
7	B	44.7 % / 31.15 %
8	B	57.1 % / 30.4 %
9	D	51.42 % / 32.29 %
10	C	32.01 % / 29.45 %
11	A	20.17 % / 28.03 %
12	B	51.14 % / 29.92 %
13	B	19.32 % / 23.67 %
14	A	17.23 % / 30.88 %
15	B	47.25 % / 26.05 %
16	C	24.05 % / 26.71 %

Q.	Ans.	Correct / Skipped
17	B	15.34 % / 32.1 %
18	D	41.19 % / 31.06 %
19	D	40.15 % / 10.32 %
20	C	38.64 % / 22.16 %
21	B	47.44 % / 22.54 %
22	A	60.61 % / 30.01 %
23	A	26.8 % / 15.25 %
24	C	23.48 % / 30.5 %
25	D	20.17 % / 32.39 %
26	A	23.58 % / 31.15 %
27	A	50.0 % / 20.83 %
28	C	31.16 % / 32.29 %
29	D	57.58 % / 23.2 %
30	B	29.55 % / 28.59 %
31	D	51.52 % / 26.98 %
32	C	42.23 % / 25.67 %

Q.	Ans.	Correct / Skipped
33	C	36.27 % / 17.23 %
34	B	12.31 % / 29.92 %
35	C	40.53 % / 26.8 %
36	D	56.44 % / 26.61 %
37	C	31.72 % / 32.01 %
38	A	32.29 % / 29.36 %
39	A	36.74 % / 31.63 %
40	A	38.73 % / 31.06 %
41	D	62.41 % / 22.72 %
42	A	44.79 % / 30.4 %
43	B	36.74 % / 26.61 %
44	C	26.04 % / 31.44 %
45	C	30.87 % / 24.05 %
46	B	37.5 % / 30.3 %
47	A	24.62 % / 27.75 %
48	C	39.2 % / 31.54 %

Q.	Ans.	Correct / Skipped
49	B	23.67 % / 33.34 %
50	B	22.82 % / 29.83 %
51	A	30.11 % / 26.71 %
52	B	47.16 % / 23.96 %
53	B	42.71 % / 32.38 %
54	C	28.22 % / 28.5 %
55	B	35.32 % / 27.18 %
56	C	20.36 % / 30.68 %
57	A	42.14 % / 31.72 %
58	D	47.73 % / 28.6 %
59	A	28.03 % / 26.89 %
60	B	11.74 % / 25.1 %
61	A	43.75 % / 31.63 %
62	C	20.36 % / 29.45 %
63	A	34.56 % / 26.99 %
64	C	11.27 % / 32.01 %

Q.	Ans.	Correct / Skipped
65	C	32.77 % / 32.0 %
66	A	18.66 % / 29.73 %
67	C	26.61 % / 31.06 %
68	C	18.47 % / 32.38 %
69	B	27.94 % / 31.91 %
70	D	10.23 % / 31.34 %
71	C	49.72 % / 16.85 %
72	B	16.19 % / 24.62 %
73	C	18.56 % / 33.33 %
74	C	29.36 % / 30.2 %
75	B	26.42 % / 31.25 %
76	B	29.07 % / 28.32 %
77	C	25.28 % / 32.77 %
78	C	19.98 % / 29.93 %
79	D	50.38 % / 18.18 %
80	C	33.33 % / 25.86 %

Q.	Ans.	Correct		Q.	Ans.	Correct		Q.	Ans.	Correct		Q.	Ans.	Correct		Q.	Ans.	Correct
		Skipped				Skipped				Skipped				Skipped				Skipped
81	A	55.87 %		89	A	22.63 %		97	C	55.3 %		105	A	52.65 %		113	A	32.48 %
		22.07 %				32.96 %				31.92 %				31.16 %				21.78 %
82	D	45.64 %		90	C	41.48 %		98	B	27.75 %		106	A	44.51 %		114	C	37.59 %
		28.22 %				31.34 %				31.06 %				31.44 %				31.44 %
83	B	12.78 %		91	C	44.32 %		99	A	50.28 %		107	C	52.08 %		115	A	24.34 %
		32.39 %				32.1 %				26.9 %				26.52 %				28.12 %
84	C	52.65 %		92	C	39.02 %		100	D	40.53 %		108	A	43.94 %		116	A	24.53 %
		28.13 %				31.53 %				26.61 %				31.44 %				31.25 %
85	C	21.12 %		93	A	26.8 %		101	B	16.67 %		109	D	23.11 %		117	A	27.27 %
		32.0 %				23.77 %				32.48 %				24.24 %				19.42 %
86	D	16.19 %		94	C	39.68 %		102	D	17.71 %		110	D	49.24 %		118	B	32.2 %
		30.31 %				32.01 %				32.57 %				30.02 %				30.87 %
87	B	55.3 %		95	D	38.26 %		103	A	23.96 %		111	B	35.32 %		119	A	17.99 %
		32.01 %				28.31 %				31.91 %				19.23 %				21.88 %
88	C	21.12 %		96	A	24.24 %		104	C	51.23 %		112	A	22.54 %		120	A	14.2 %
		31.82 %				28.13 %				28.32 %				30.87 %				25.0 %

Performance Analysis	
Avg. Score (%)	34.0%
Toppers Score (%)	100.0%
Your Score	

//Hints and Solutions//

1. E-commerce means availing all the business over the net. E-commerce (electronic commerce) is the buying and selling of goods and services, or the transmitting of funds or data, over an electronic network, primarily the internet. These business transactions occur either as business-to-business (B2B), business-to-consumer (B2C), consumer-to-consumer, or consumer-to-business.
Hence, the correct option is (D).

2. In process of online banking transactions are entered through the terminal and then they are recorded, verified, authenticated, and corresponding updations are reflected instantly.
Hence, the correct option is (C).

3. Software programs and computer peripherals both come under computerized accounting.
A computerized accounting system is an accounting information system that processes financial transactions and events as per Generally Accepted Accounting Principles (GAAP) to produce reports as per user requirements.
Hence, the correct option is (D).

4. Computer programming is a process that leads from an original formulation of a computing problem to executable computer programs.
Input is the process of entering data and instructions into the computer. The process of entering data and instructions into the computer is called data entry, coding, or programming. Input devices, output devices, and CPU are three essential hardware, these three can't be called Processes.
Hence, the correct option is (C).

5. The twentieth century has been the century of the advent of-
Internet- A global computer network providing a variety of information and communication facilities, consisting of interconnected networks using standardized communication protocols.**E-mail**- An e-mail is a message sent from one computer to another over the Internet, using a set webmail server address.**E-commerce**- Electronic commerce or e-commerce (sometimes written as eCommerce) is a business model that lets firms and individuals buy and sell things over the internet.
Hence, the correct option is (D).

6. Issued capital is taken up by the general public. Such capital can be offered to the public at a later date. It is that part of subscribed capital, which is called by the company to pay on shares allotted. It is not necessary for the company to call for the entire amount on shares subscribed for by shareholders.
Hence, the correct option is (A).

7. Under online processing, the majority of transactions are processed online.
Online processing is the ongoing entry of transactions into a computer system in real-time. The opposite of this system is batch processing, where transactions are allowed to pile up in a stack of documents and are entered into the computer system in a batch.
Hence, the correct option is (B).

8. CRM stands for Customer Relationship Management.
Customer relationship management (CRM) is the combination of practices, strategies, and technologies that companies use to manage and analyze customer interactions and data throughout the customer lifecycle, with the goal of improving customer service relationships and assisting in customer retention, and driving sales.
Hence, the correct option is (B).

9. Issues that banks face in today's hyper-competitive environment:
1-Consumer expectations.
2-Increasing pressure from competition.
3-Investor expectations.
4-Regulatory conditions.
Hence, the correct option is (D).

10. Capital budgeting, and investment appraisal, is the planning process used to determine whether an organization's long term investments such as new machinery, replacement of machinery, new plants, new products, and research development projects are worth the funding of cash through the firm's capitalization structure (debt, equity or retained earnings). It is the process of allocating resources for major capital, or investment, expenditures. One of the primary goals of capital budgeting investments is to increase the value of the firm to the shareholders.

Hence, the correct option is (C).

11. Sales can be calculated by preparing the Debtor Account:

Sundry Debtors Account

Particulars	Amount	Particulars	Amount
To opening Balance B/f	10200	By Cash	30400
To credit Sales	**37900**	By Return Inwards	2700
		By Bad Debts	1200
		By Closing Balance c/f	13800
Total	**48100**	**Total**	**48100**
Cash Sales (A)	28400		
Cash Sales (B)	37900	**Total sales(A+B)**	**66300**

Hence, the correct option is (A).

12. A cheque returned by bank marked "NSF" means that there are not sufficient funds in your account. Non-sufficient funds (NSF) is a term used in the banking industry to indicate that a cheque cannot be honoured because insufficient funds are available in the account on which the instrument was drawn.
Hence, the correct option is (B).

13. 84,000 - 4,000 + 1,500 (Not recorded as profit) + 1500 (because it was rated as an expense).
Therefore, the amount of 1,500 discount will be added two times = Rs. 83,000
Hence, the correct option is (B).

14. The given statement is true.
In order to arrive at the balance sheet of a business, one needs to prepare the trading account and profit and loss account first. This account is prepared to arrive at the figure for revenue earned or loss incurred during a period.
Hence, the correct option is (A).

15. 2,00,000 - 60,000 = 1,40,000

2% discount on the balance = $140{,}000 \times 2\%$

$$= 140{,}000 \times \frac{2}{100} = 2{,}800$$

Final balance payable = 1,40,000 - 2,800 = 1,37,200
Hence, the correct option is (B).

16. Accounts payable (creditors) carry a credit balance. Hence, a reserve created on creditors will be debited and P & L a/c would be credited against it.

Reserve for Discount on Accounts Payable A/c - To Profit & Loss A/c
Hence, the correct option is (C).

17. Mutually exclusive projects are projects in which acceptance of one project excludes the others from consideration. In such a scenario, the best project is accepted. NPV and IRR conflict, which can sometimes arise in the case of mutually exclusive projects, becomes critical. The conflict either arises due to the relative size of the project or due to the different cash flow distribution of the projects. Since NPV is an absolute measure, it will rank a project adding more dollar value higher regardless of the original investment required. IRR is a relative measure, and it will rank projects offering the best investment return higher regardless of the total value-added.
Hence, the correct option is (B).

18. Depreciation means a decline in the book value of assets. The assets generally have a useful life for more than one accounting period. Assets have a limited useful life. Assets are used to earn income by way of rent, for production of goods or services, or for office use.

If the product is used for purpose of resale then it can not be called an asset as it is for trade.

Hence, the correct option is (D).

19. The accounting rate of return, also known as the average rate of return, or ARR is a financial ratio used in capital budgeting. ARR calculates the return generated from the net income of the proposed capital investment.

$$\text{Accounting Rate of Return Formula} = \frac{\text{Average Annual Profit}}{\text{Initial Investment}}$$

Hence, the correct option is (D).

20. Diversification is a technique that reduces risk by allocating investments among various financial instruments, industries, and other categories. It aims to maximize returns by investing in different areas that would each react differently to the same event.
Hence, the correct option is (C).

21. Suppose Rs.100 is invested. The rate per annum is 10%, i.e. 5% per half-year. The amount after the first half-year will be 100 + 5%, i.e. Rs. 105 and amount after second half-year, i.e. one year will be 105 + 5%, i.e. Rs. 110.25. Thus, the effective rate of interest per annum is 110.25 - 100 = 10.25%.
Hence, the correct option is (B).

22. RTGS helps in the transfer of money and securities from one bank to another.
The term real-time gross settlement (RTGS) refers to a funds transfer system that allows for the instantaneous transfer of money and/or securities.
Hence, the correct option is (A).

23. Correct entry would have been subtracting the amount from the passbook, but as the amount has been recorded twice, it means the amount has been subtracted twice, so the amount will be added once to nullify the difference.
Hence, the correct option is (A).

24. Credit transfer is a direct payment of money from one bank account to another. The other options are to be debited, not credited.
Hence, the correct option is (C).

25. The bank balance which is shown in the balance sheet of an organization is the balance after matching it with the cash book.
The balance sheet includes-
Assets: Cash, marketable securities, prepaid expenses, accounts receivable, inventory, and fixed assets.
Liabilities: Accounts payable, accrued liabilities, customer prepayments, taxes payable, short-term debt, and long-term debt.
Hence, the correct option is (D).

26. The entry will be passed in the cash book after it is posted in the passbook.
A cheque received may be deposited into the bank on the same day or on another day. The amount is recorded in the bank column of the cash book on the receipts side in case the cheque is deposited on the same day.
Hence, the correct option is (A).

27. Passbook a book issued by a bank or building society to an account holder, recording sums deposited and withdrawn.
The passbook is just a copy of the account statement as maintained by the bank. So if the passbook reflects a debit balance it means that the account is in the nature of a debtor/receivable for the bank and it would be the opposite for the account holder.
Hence, the correct option is (A).

28. The bank credits the account when the bank credits the amount in the account. On the other hand, when the bank deducts any amount from your account, it debits the account.
Hence, the correct option is (C).

29. The first two entries create a difference between the entries made in the cash book and the entries made by the bank. The third entry where the cheques have been deposited by the customer is added in the cash book and credited by the bank, i.e. added in the passbook. So, this entry will not show any difference.
Hence, the correct option is (D).

30. The reconciliation is as follows-

Particulars	Amount in Rs.
Balance as per pass book(Cr.)	20000
Add cheque deposited but not credited by the	15000

bank	
add bank charges not entered in the cash book	100
Balance as per cash book(Dr.)	35100

Hence, the correct option is (B).

31. The bank reconciliation book is to find if there is any mismatch between the cash book and bank passbook. If there is so, then it is useful in finding the reason for the mismatch and correcting it.
For reconciling the balances as shown in the Cash Book and passbook a reconciliation statement is prepared known as Bank Reconciliation Statement or BRS. In other words, BRS is a statement that is prepared for reconciling the difference between balances as per the cash book's bank column and passbook on a given date.
Hence, the correct option is (D).

32. KYC procedures defined by banks involve all the necessary actions to make sure their customers are real, assess, and monitor risks. These processes help prevent and identify money laundering, terrorism financing, and other illegal corruption schemes.

KYC process includes ID card verification, face verification, document verification such as utility bills as proof of address, and biometric verification.

Banks must comply with KYC regulations and anti-money laundering regulations to limit fraud. KYC compliance responsibility rests with the banks.

Hence, the correct option is (C).

33. The debt/equity ratio is a debt ratio used to measure a company's financial leverage. It is calculated by dividing a company's total liabilities by its stockholders' equity. Therefore, it is considered good when it is 2:1.
Hence, the correct option is (C).

34. The payout ratio is the percentage of net income that a company pays out as dividends to common shareholders. The ratio is calculated as the percentage of earnings paid out as dividends.
Hence, the correct option is (B).

35. Proprietary Ratio = $\dfrac{Shareholder's\ Fund}{Total\ Assets}$
The proprietary ratio is also known as the equity ratio. It helps to determine the financial strength of a company & is useful for creditors to assess the ratio of shareholders' funds employed out of total assets of the company. Proprietors' funds are also known as Owners' funds, shareholders' funds, Net Worth, etc.
Hence, the correct option is (C).

36. The debtor collection period is different in different types of industries. It also differs according to the terms and conditions of the policy and the nature of the product.
An average collection period shows the average number of days necessary to convert business receivables into cash. The degree to which this is useful for a business depends on the relative reliance on credit sales by the company to generate revenue – a high balance in accounts receivable can be a major liability.
Hence, the correct option is (D).

37. The operating ratio is a financial term defined as a company's operating expenses as a percentage of revenue.

Operating Ratio = $\dfrac{Operating\ Expense}{Net\ Sales}$

Hence, the correct option is (C).

38. Capital Employed = Total Assets - Current Liabilities

= Fixed Assets + Current Assets - Current Liabilities

= Fixed Assets + Working Capital
Hence, the correct option is (A).

39. Profitability is a measure of efficiency and the search for it provides an incentive to achieve efficiency. Profitability ratios can be determined on the basis of either sales or investments. The profitability ratios in relation to sales are-

(a) Profit margin (gross and net),

(b) Expenses ratio or operating ratio.
Hence, the correct option is (A).

40. Long term solvency is judged by the ratios like debt-equity ratio, proprietary ratio, total assets to debt ratio.
This way, the solvency ratio assesses a company's long-term health by evaluating its repayment ability for its long-term debt and the interest on that debt. As a general rule of thumb, a solvency ratio higher than 20% is considered to be financially sound, however, solvency ratios vary from industry to industry.
Hence, the correct option is (A).

41. Ratios act as indicators of the good position of the company because it shows the financial position of the company. If a company is sound, it will ultimately result in a good position and strength.
Efficiency ratios measure the efficiency of the company in turning over inventory, receivables, or payables. Leverage ratios indicate the long-term solvency of the company. Liquidity and Efficiency Ratios: Current ratio (current assets ÷ current liabilities): The higher, the more liquid the company is.
Hence, the correct option is (D).

42. Window dressing means the actions taken to improve the appearance of a company's financial statements. Window dressing is particularly common when a business has a large number of shareholders, so that management can give the appearance of a well-run company to investors who probably do not have much day-to-day contact with the business.
Hence, the correct option is (A).

43. The provision for doubtful debts is an account receivable contra account, so it should always have a credit balance.

Therefore, entry for provision for bad debts is:

Profit and Loss a/c Dr To Provision for bad and doubtful debt.
Hence, the correct option is (B).

44. $2,00,000 \times \left(\dfrac{20}{100}\right)$
$= Rs.\ 40,000$
1st year value =
$2,00,000 - 40,000$
$= Rs.\ 1,60,000$

2nd years value

$$1,60,000 - 40,000$$
$$= Rs.\,1,20,000$$

Hence, the correct option is (C).

45. A rights issue is a dividend of subscription rights to buy additional securities in a company made to the company's existing security holders.
A rights issue is an invitation to existing shareholders to purchase additional new shares in the company. This type of issue gives existing shareholders securities called rights. With the rights, the shareholder can purchase new shares at a discount to the market price on a stated future date.
Hence, the correct option is (C).

46. The minimum tradable lot is decided according to the existing provision which is contained in the SEBI.
After the incorporation of the company, the company needs to issue the share certificates within two months from the incorporation date. Where additional shares are allotted to the new or existing shareholders, the share certificates should be issued within two months from the allotment date.
Hence, the correct option is (B).

47. Share application money is the amount received by a company from applicants who wish to purchase its shares. It is the money received with respect to an initial public offering of shares. This money can be more or less than the actual amount anticipated with respect to the number of shares floated.
Hence, the correct option is (A).

48. Under the head Issued Capital should be stated if the shares are issued, then all the classes of shares. If it's preference share, then all the sub-classes of preference share should be stated.
Hence, the correct option is (C).

49. Total profit- Rs. 100.

After paying to charity, A's share = Rs. $95 \times \dfrac{3}{5} = Rs.\,57.$

If A's share is Rs.57, total profit = Rs.100.

If A's share Rs.855, total profit = $\dfrac{100}{57} \times 855 = 1500.$

Hence, the correct option is (B).

50. Balance Sheet is prepared as per Part I Schedule III.
Section 129 of the companies act in 2013, provides for the preparation of financial statements. 2(40) to include a balance sheet, profit and loss account/income and expenditure account, cash flow statement, statement of changes in equity, and any explanatory note annexed to the above.
Hence, the correct option is (B).

51. X acquired= Rs. 7,50,000 assets
Issue of shares= Rs. 100

The number of shares to be issued by X Ltd= $\dfrac{750000}{125}$ = 6,000 shares
Hence, the correct option is (A).

52. Statutory corporations are public enterprises brought into existence by a Special Act of the Parliament. The Act defines its powers and functions, rules, and regulations governing its employees and its relationship with government departments.
Hence, the correct option is (B).

53. The expansion of CAPM is a Capital asset, pricing model. The capital asset pricing model (CAPM) is used to calculate the required rate of return for any risky asset.

Hence, the correct option is (B).

54. A Public Company is a company whose shares are traded freely on a stock exchange and the minimum number of directors is 3.
The 1956 Act prescribed a minimum of 2 directors for a private and 3 for a public company respectively to constitute a Board. This criterion has been retained by the new Act, but the maximum limit of directors on the Board has now been raised from 12 to 15.
Hence, the correct option is (C).

55. Errors of principle may occur due to the wrong allocation between capital and revenue expenditure, or wrong valuation of assets.
Repairs to buildings are debited to Buildings Account is an error of principle.
Hence, the correct option is (B).

56. The errors which are committed while recording or posting a transaction are called errors of commission. Such errors include posting wrong amounts, posting on the wrong side of accounts or posting in wrong accounts, wrong totaling or carrying forward, and wrong balancing.
Hence, the correct option is (C).

57. A suspense account is an account in the books of an organization in which items are entered temporarily before allocation to the correct or final account.
A suspense account is a catch-all section of a general ledger used by companies to record ambiguous entries that require clarification. Suspense accounts are routinely cleared out once the nature of the suspended amounts are resolved, and are subsequently shuffled to their correctly designated accounts.
Hence, the correct option is (A).

58. A trial balance contains balances of all the accounts.
A trial balance is a list of all the general ledger accounts (both revenue and capital) contained in the ledger of a business. This list will contain the name of each nominal ledger account and the value of that nominal ledger balance. Each nominal ledger account will hold either a debit balance or a credit balance.
Hence, the correct option is (D).

59. Trial balance is a statement of all debits and credits in a double-entry accounts book, with any disagreement indicating an error.

A trial balance is a list of all the general ledger accounts (both revenue and capital) contained in the ledger of a business. This list will contain the name of each nominal ledger account and the value of that nominal ledger balance. Each nominal ledger account will hold either a debit balance or a credit balance.

Hence, the correct option is (A).

60. It means that the purchases have been reduced to the extent of the stock amount at the end of the period.

11 January 2011 If closing stock appeared in Trial balance it means the purchases have been reduced to the extent of the stock amount at the end of the period.
Hence, the correct option is (B).

61. Net working capital is a liquidity calculation that measures a company's ability to pay off its current liabilities with current assets.

Hence, the correct option is (A).

62. Short term sources are Commercial papers. Commercial paper is a money-market security issued (sold) by large corporations to obtain funds to meet short-term debt obligations (for example, payroll) and is backed only by an issuing bank or company promise to pay the face amount on the maturity date specified on the note.

Hence the correct option is (C).

63. Capital expenditure is money invested by a company to acquire or upgrade fixed, physical, non-consumable assets, such as buildings and equipment or a new business.
Hence, the correct option is (A).

64. Mutual accommodation means both the persons will receive half the amount, i.e. 10,000.

Charges for discounting = 12% per annum

We need to find for 2 months, which will come out to be Rs. 200.

Rs. 200 will also be divided equally as charges.

Therefore, B's receivables will be 5,000 - 100 = 4,900.
Hence, the correct option is (C).

65. The amount of the bill would be

10,000 + 200 (for bank charges) = Rs. 10,200.

Hence, the correct option is (C).

66. The arbitrary process is the behavioral foundation for the MM approach. The MM approach favors the Net operating income approach and agrees with the fact that the cost of capital is independent of the degree of leverage and at any mix of debt-equity proportions.

Hence, the correct option is (A).

67. The endorsement is the direct transfer of rights on the bill from the drawer to the creditors.

Endorsement of the bill implies the procedure by which the maker or holder of the bill transfers the title of the bill in assistance of his/her creditors. The individual transferring the title is called "Endorser" and the individual to whom the bill is exchanged called "Endorsee".
Hence, the correct option is (C).

68. The Combined Leverage (CL) is not a distinct type of leverage analysis, rather it is a product of the Operating Leverage and the Financial Leverage. The CL may be defined as the % change in EPS for a given % change in the sales level and may be calculated as follows:

Combined Leverage = Operating Leverage x Financial Leverage = $\dfrac{\%\ Change\ in\ EPS}{\%\ Change\ in\ sales}$
Hence, the correct option is (C).

69. The maturity date is the date when the bill gets matured or the day when payment becomes due.
Maturity means the date on which a bill of exchange falls due for payment. The date of maturity is to be calculated in respect of bills which are payable after a specified time.
Hence, the correct option is (B).

70. Bills payable discounted in the cash by the creditor need not be recorded.
No entry is required because that entry will be recorded in the books of accounts of that creditor.
Hence, the correct option is (D).

71. There are 3 parties involved in payment by bill of exchange:

1. Drawer
2. Drawee
3. Payee

The drawer is the party that issues a bill of exchange – the 'creditor'; the beneficiary or payee is the party to which the bill of exchange is payable; the drawee is the party to which the order to pay is sent - 'the debtor'.

Hence, the correct option is (C).

72. A company's cost of capital is simply the cost of money the company uses for financing. If a company only uses current liabilities and long-term debt to finance its operations, then it uses debt and the cost of capital is usually the interest rate on that debt. The cost of capital is also called the hurdle rate.

Hence, the correct option is (B).

73. Calculation of Capital balance in the beginning:

Particulars	Ram	Mohan
Capitals at the end of the year	24000	18000
Less: Profit already credited	(8000)	(8000)
Add: Drawings already debited	4000	6000
Capital at the beginning of the year	20000	16000

Note: Interest on capital is always calculated on the opening balance of the partner's capital.

Ram's interest in capital = $20000 \times \dfrac{5}{100}$

= 1000

Mohan's interest on capital = $16000 \times \dfrac{5}{100}$

= 800

Hence, the correct option is (C).

74. Solution to the given problem can be given through the below equation:
Opening Capital + Capital Introduced + Profit - Drawings = Closing Capital
By putting the information:
Opening Capital + Rs.5000 - Rs.10000 (Loss) - Rs.8000 = Rs.7000

Opening Capital - Rs.13000 = Rs.7000
Opening Capital = Rs.7000 + Rs.13000
Opening Capital = Rs.20000
Hence, the correct option is (C).

75. Net profit is the gross profit (revenue minus COGS) minus operating expenses and all other expenses, such as taxes and interest paid on debt. Although it may appear more complicated, net profit is calculated for us and provided on the income statement as net income.

Net Profit is the actual profit after working expenses not included in the calculation of gross profit has been paid.

Hence, the correct option is (B).

76. As per the prudence concept, do not overestimate the number of revenues recognized or underestimate the number of expenses.
Prudence Concept or Conservatism principle is a key accounting principle that makes sure that assets and income are not overstated and provision is made for all known expenses and losses whether the amount is known for certain or just an estimation.
Hence, the correct option is (B).

77. Provision for bad debts is made as per the Conservatism concept. The conservatism principle is the general concept of recognizing expenses and liabilities as soon as possible when there is uncertainty about the outcome, but only recognize revenues and assets when they are assured of being received.

Going concern concept assumes that business will be carried on for an INDEFINITE period.

Capital losses need to be deducted to ascertain net income.

The materiality concept states that transactions of insignificant value need not be recorded.

Hence, the correct option is (C).

78. An important concept of accrual accounting, the matching principle states that the related revenues and expenses must be matched in the same period. This is done in order to link the costs of an asset or revenue to its benefits.

Accrual Concept: Financial statements are prepared under the Accruals Concept of accounting which requires that income and expense must be recognized in the accounting periods to which they relate rather than on a cash basis.

Accounting conservatism is a principle that requires company accounts to be prepared with caution and high degrees of verification. All probable losses are recorded when they are discovered, while gains can only be registered when they are fully realized.

The sole purpose of the consistency principle, or consistency concept, is to ensure that transactions or events are recorded in the same way, from one accounting year to the next. In other words, businesses should not use a certain accounting method one year, and a different accounting method the next year.

The realization principle is the concept that revenue can only be recognized once the underlying goods or services associated with the revenue have been delivered or rendered, respectively. Thus, revenue can only be recognized after it has been earned.

Hence, the correct option is (C).

79. Savings accounts are liquid but are not marketable. Marketable securities and money market holdings are considered cash equivalents because they are liquid and not subject to material fluctuations in value.

Hence, the correct option is (D).

80. The separate entity concept is the basic accounting concept which states that we should always separately record the transactions of a business and its owners.

Double entry, a fundamental concept underlying present-day bookkeeping and accounting, states that every financial transaction has equal and opposite effects in at least two different accounts.

Going concerned, is an accounting term for a company that has the resources needed to continue operating indefinitely until it provides evidence to the contrary. ... If a business is not a **going concern,** it **means** it's **gone** bankrupt and its assets were liquidated.

In accounting, **materiality** refers to the relative size of an amount. Relatively large amounts are material, while relatively small amounts are not material (or immaterial). Determining **materiality** requires professional judgment.

Hence, the correct option is (C).

81. Nominal accounts in accounting are temporary accounts, such as the income statement accounts. In other words, nominal accounts are the accounts that report revenues, expenses, gains, and losses.

A **Nominal account** is a General ledger **account pertaining** to all income, expenses, losses, and gains. An example of a **Nominal Account** is an Interest **Account**.

Hence, the correct option is (A).

82. The three column cash book represents Real, personal and nominal accounts. The three column cash book (also known as triple column cash book) has three money columns on both debit and credit side – one on each side for recording discount, cash and bank amounts.
Hence, the correct option is (D).

83. Purchases and Sales can be treated as either nominal accounts or real accounts.

GOLDEN RULE: "Debit all expenses and losses, Credit all incomes and gains."
Hence, the correct option is (B).

84. A journal (daybook, a book of original entry) is a place for recording transactions as they occur. Journal entries are the first step in the accounting cycle.
Journals are also referred to as books of original entries. The information in these books is then summarized and posted into a general ledger, from which financial statements are produced.
Hence, the correct option is (C).

85. A ledger holds account information that is needed to prepare financial statements and includes accounts for assets, liabilities, owner's equity, revenues, and expenses.
The ledger contains information that is required to prepare financial statements. It includes accounts for assets, liabilities, owner's equity, revenues, and expenses. This complete list of accounts is known as the chart of accounts. The ledger represents every active account on the list.
Hence, the correct option is (C).

86. A cash book is a financial journal that contains all cash receipts and payments, including bank deposits and withdrawals.

In the given case, no cash is received. therefore, there will be no entry in the cash book.

Hence, the correct option is (D).

87. A cash book is a financial journal that contains all cash receipts and payments, including bank deposits and withdrawals.
Hence, the correct option is (B).

88. Under the imprest system, an amount is given to a petty cashier to meet expenses during a period. At the end of the period, he is given cash equal to the amount spent during the relevant period, if this adjusting entry is not made, the cash balance in the main cash book is overstated to the extent of the expenses routed through the petty cash book and the expenses are unstated.

Hence, the correct option is (C).

89. Leading and lagging and extension of trade credit:

Leading: it implies speeding up collections on receivables if the foreign currency in which they are invoiced is expected to appreciate.

Lagging: it implies delaying payments of payables invoiced in a foreign currency that is expected to depreciate.

Netting is a process by which exposure or obligation is reduced by combining two or more positions. The value of multiple positions is analyzed and offset, and eventually, the parties that need to be paid and pay are determined. Multilateral netting involves more than two parties.

Hence, the correct option is (A).

90. Cross rates are the relation of two currencies against each other, based on the rate of each of them against a third currency. For example, the Bank of England sells or purchases euros for yen. To calculate the cross rate of the EURJPY, the bank will use the dollar quotes for the two pairs, EURUSD and USDJPY.
Hence, the correct option is (C).

91. The spot market or cash market is a public financial market in which financial instruments or commodities are traded for immediate delivery. It is opposite to the futures market in which delivery is due at a later date.

Hence, the correct option is (C).

92. Foreign Exchange Market is also known as over the counter (OTC) and interbank.
The foreign exchange market – also called forex, FX, or currency market – was one of the original financial markets formed to bring structure to the burgeoning global economy. In terms of trading volume, it is, by far, the largest financial market in the world.
Hence, the correct option is (C).

93. AS 7 deals with accounting for construction contracts in the financial statements of enterprises undertaking such contracts (hereafter referred to as 'contractors').
The statement also applies to enterprises undertaking construction activities of the type dealt with in this statement not as contractors but on their own account as a venture of a commercial nature where the enterprise has entered into agreements for sale.
Hence, the correct option is (A).

94. AS 28 should be applied in accounting for impairment of all assets except options A and B because they are not considered under assets. They are considered under inventories.
Hence, the correct option is (C).

95. AS 11 requires the enterprise to disclose-
1-The amount of exchange differences including the net profit or loss for the period.
2-The amount of exchange differences adjusted in the carrying amount of fixed assets.
3-The amount of exchange differences in respect of forwarding exchange contracts to be recognized in the profit or loss in one or more subsequent accounting period (over the life of the contract).
Hence, the correct option is (D).

96. AS 4 deals with treatment in the financial statements of:
(A) Contingencies.
(B) Events that occur after the balance sheet date.
The followings that might result in the contingencies are excluded from the scope of AS 4 bearing in mind special considerations which are applicable to them:
(a) Liabilities of general insurance enterprises and life assurance which arises from the insurance policies issued.
(b) Commitments which arise from a long-term lease contract.
(c) Obligations under a retirement benefit plan.
Hence, the correct option is (A).

97. Accounting Standards (ASs) are written policy documents issued by an expert accounting body or by the government or other regulatory body covering the aspects of recognition, measurement, presentation, and disclosure of accounting transactions in the financial statements.

Accounting Standards provide an essential supporting structure and standard accounting policies. So, both the options are correct.

Hence, the correct option is (C).

98. Accounting standards set the trend towards rigidity and eliminate flexibility which can prove a disadvantage sometimes.
Hence, the correct option is (B).

99. The Institute of Chartered Accountants of India (ICAI) constituted the Accounting Standards Boards (ASB) on 21st April 1977 to harmonize the diverse accounting policies and practices in the use of India. ASB of the ICIA has been issuing accounting standards.

Since then, it has issued 32 Accounting Standards
Hence, the correct option is (A).

100. Accounting standards are written policy documents issued by expert accounting bodies or by government or regulatory bodies covering the aspects of recognition, treatment, measurement, presentation, and disclosure of accounting transactions and events in the financial statements.
Hence, the correct option is (D).

101. The American Accounting Association promotes accounting education, research, and practice. Founded in 1916 as the American Association of University Instructors in Accounting, its present name was adopted in 1936. The Association is a voluntary group of persons interested in accounting education and research.
Hence, the correct option is (B).

102. The present value at 8% p.a. for 15 years from the standard table is 8.5525 which multiplied by 15,000 amounts to Rs. 1,28,288 approx.
Hence, the correct option is (D).

103. When a company uses debt funds in its financial structure, it will lead to a change in financial leverage. Financial leverage is the amount of debt that an entity uses to buy more assets. Leverage is employed to avoid using too much equity to fund operations.
Hence, the correct option is (A).

104. Future value = present value × [1 + (interest rate × time)]

Interest = 50,000 $\times$ 5.5 $\times$ $\dfrac{2}{100}$ = Rs. 5500

Interest = 5500

Amount = 50000 + 5500 = Rs. 55,500
Hence, the correct option is (C).

105. A bank is a financial institution that accepts deposits from the public and creates credit. Lending activities can be performed either directly or indirectly through capital markets.
Hence, the correct option is (A).

106. A Performing Asset is something that you own that pays you a flow of money on a regular basis. Cash flow. Regular payments. The money you can use to live your life, month to month! A good Performing Asset is as reliable as your salary.
Hence, the correct option is (A).

107. For banks, printing and stationery expenses include the cost of stationery items which are used daily in offices, and the printed material for correspondence purposes.
For example business letterheads, business cards, envelopes, etc.
Hence, the correct option is (C).

108. General Ledger(GL) accounts contain all debit and credit transactions. The account reflected on a trial balance are related to all major accounting items, including assets, liabilities, equity, revenues, expenses, gain, and losses
Hence, the correct option is (A).

109. Discount allowed by a seller is a loss since he is receiving a lesser amount than what he could have received without allowing a discount.

Hence, at the time of receiving the payment, the discount allowed is recorded in the 'Discount' column on the debit side (or receipts side) of the Double Column Cash Book (with cash and discount columns).

This statement also holds valid in the case of Triple Column Cash Book (with cash, discount, and blank columns).

Hence, the correct option is (D).

110. According to the RBI, those categorised as low-risk customers should be asked to update KYC details once in 10 years, for medium risk once in 8 years and for high-risk customers once in two years. This would involve providing identification and address proof. Customers who are minors have to submit a fresh photograph on becoming major.
Hence, the correct option is (D).

111. Both sales and X Ltd. accounts are understated by Rs. 900. Entries are required to increase the amount due from X Ltd. And increase sales by crediting the sales account.
Hence, the correct option is (B).

112. Marketable securities are primarily short-term debt instruments. Marketable securities are securities or debts that are to be sold or redeemed within a year. These are financial instruments that can be easily converted to cash such as government bonds, common stock, or certificates of deposit.

Hence, the correct option is (A).

113. Bonus shares are not permitted unless the partly paid shares, if any, are made fully-paid. Bonus shares are shares distributed by a company to its current shareholders as fully paid shares free of charge.
Hence, the correct option is (A).

114. Cash is received, so it would be debited (3600 - 54 = 3546). Discount is a loss since the payment is received after deducting it. Hence, it would also be debited.

Discount = 3,600 $\times$ $\dfrac{6}{100}$ $\times$ $\dfrac{3}{12}$ = Rs. 54.

B/R has gone out, so it would be credited.
Hence, the correct option is (C).

115. Interest on drawings is an income for the business, so it will be credited. And it will be charged from the capital account of partners, so the Capital account will be credited.

Capital A/c Dr 1,200

To Interest on drawings a/c 1,200

Hence, the correct option is (A).

116. Bad debts are a loss and loss is always debited. Since debtors is an asset, and it has decreased, which means it has gone out, so we would credit debtors.

Bad debts A/c Dr 770

To debtor's A/c 770
Hence, the correct option is (A).

117. The basic assumptions or conditions upon the edifice on which the accounting superstructure is based are called accounting concepts.

The accounting concept refers to the basic assumptions and rules and principles which work as the basis of recording business transactions and preparing accounts. This concept assumes that, for accounting purposes, the business enterprise and its owners are two separate independent entities.

Hence, the correct option is (A).

118. Net income available to stockholders = 125

Total assets = 1,096

Return on common equity rate shows the net income earned per every rupee invested. It acts as a yardstick of profitability.

Return on common equity =
$$\frac{(net\ income - preferential\ stock)}{Average\ common\ stock\ holder's\ equity}$$

No further information is available

$$= \left(\frac{125}{1096}\right) \times 100$$

= 11.4051 %
Hence, the correct option is (B).

119. Return on Equity (ROE) = Net Profit Margin $\times$ Asset Turnover Ratio $\times$ Equity Multiplier.

$$= 4.5\% \times 2.2 \times 2.7$$

= 26.73%
Hence, the correct option is (A).

120. If a fixed amount is withdrawn on the last day of every month of the calendar year, the interest on the total amount of drawings will be calculated for 5.5 months.

The average period will be calculated as = Months left after first drawing + months left after the last drawing

$$= \frac{11 + 0}{2}$$

= 5.5 months.

If drawings are made on the first day of the month, interest is charged for 6.5 months, and for the mid of every month, the time period is 6 months.

Hence, the correct option is (A).

Q.1 ATMs are capable of

A. accepting cash/cheque

B. disbursing cash

C. making inter-bank transfer

D. All of the above

Q.2 Compilation of related data records maintained in some pre-arranged order is known as

A. database

B. data file

C. data mart

D. data group

Q.3 A multiple user computer system is beneficial because

A. It connects several computers through LAN or WAN.

B. More than one person can share the work of data feeding simultaneously.

C. Each user can handle particular segment of a transaction.

D. All of the above

Q.4 Core bank component includes

(i) financial institution infrastructure

(ii) product build

(iii) customers management and customers overview

(iv) account administration

(v) payments

(vi) management information

A. (i), (ii), (iii) and (iv)

B. (ii), (iii), (iv) and (v)

C. (iii), (iv), (v) and (vi)

D. All of the above

Q.5 The concept of automated banking through Automated Teller machines (ATMs) is the result of

A. Computerisation

B. Technological innovation

C. Both (A) and (B)

D. None of the above

Q.6 _______ is a compilation of related data records maintained in some pre-arranged order.

A. Data **B.** Record **C.** Data file **D.** System

Q.7 _______ are mostly used in scientific and mechanical fields and they provide data in a continuous form.

A. Analog computers

B. Digital computers

C. Both (A) and (B)

D. None of the above

Q.8 The purpose of accounting is to provide information used in

A. Planning

B. Decision making

C. Organizing

D. Controlling

Q.9 Sundry debtors on 31st March, 2006 are Rs. 55,200. Further bad debts are Rs. 200. Provision for doubtful debts is to be made on debtors at the rate of 5% and also, provision of discount is to be made on debtors at the rate of 2%. The amount of provision of doubtful debts will be

A. Rs. 1,045

B. Rs. 2,750

C. Rs. 1,100

D. Rs. 2,760

Q.10 A company limited by shares can issue _____.

A. Equity shares

B. Preference shares

C. Equity and preference both shares

D. None of the above

Q.11 _______ deals with accounting for investments.

A. AS 11 **B.** AS 12 **C.** AS 13 **D.** AS 14

Q.12 At the end of the year 2008-09, the ledger of a firm shows the following balances in their balance sheet:

Capital	2,00,000
Profit for the year	1,50,000
Provision for tax	75,000
Liabilities	1,00,000
Advance tax paid	60,000
Sundry assets	4,65,000

The total balance sheet would be

A. Rs. 4,65,000

B. Rs. 5,25,000

C. Rs. 5,65,000

D. Rs. 5,10,000

Q.13 The following details relate to a trading concern for the year 2010:

Opening stock Rs. 4,000. Purchases and sales during the year Rs. 36,000 and Rs. 35,000, respectively. Profit on sales is 20%. 50% of the closing stock was found to be obsolete and estimated to fetch only 50% of cost. The value for the closing stock at the end of the year will be

A. Rs. 9,000

B. Rs. 12,000

C. Rs. 6,000

D. Rs. 10,500

Q.14 Somnath Enterprises wishes to earn a 20% profit margin on selling price. How much should they charge on cost to achieve the required margin?

A. 50% **B.** 33% **C.** 25% **D.** 20%

Q.15 Mr. Rishi sells goods at 20% above cost. His sales were Rs. 10,20,000 during the year. However, he sold damaged goods for Rs. 20,000 costing Rs. 30,000. This sale is included in Rs. 10,20,000. The amount of gross profit is

A. Rs. 1,90,000

B. Rs. 2,50,000

C. Rs. 1,56,667

D. Rs. 2,00,000

Q.16 Sensitivity analysis for NPV determination identifies

A. Areas of concern in an investment opportunity

B. Those factors which are sensitive to the profitability of the investment opportunity

C. Those areas where more efforts are required to be made to explore more information

D. All of the above

Q.17 Which of the following is/are the advantage(s) of NPV and IRR methods?
A. They give exact results
B. They take into account time value of money
C. They focus on cash flows rather than on accounting profits
D. Both (B) and (C)

Q.18 Internal rate of return is the rate of _________ in NPV equation at which the present value of cash flows of a project equals its initial outlay.
A. cash flow
B. investment
C. discount
D. years

Q.19 Time value of money means
A. A sum of money received today has more value than the same amount of money to be received in future because the money received today can be invested today to get some more earning.
B. Since there is risk involved in future, an individual would always like to receive money today than to wait for the future and be under risk.
C. The money received today can be used for any consumption which one may not be able to do because of future inflation and price rise.
D. All of the above

Q.20 A project requires an initial investment of Rs. 20,000 with annual cashflow of Rs. 4,000. Compute the pay-back period.
A. 5 years
B. 9 years
C. 10 years
D. 16 years

Q.21 A bond of face value Rs. 5,000 carries a coupon interest rate of 12%. It is quoted in the market at Rs. 4,500. What is the current yield of the bond?
A. 12%
B. 10%
C. 13.3%
D. 14.2%

Q.22 Debit balance as per cash book is Rs. 3,000. Cheque issued but not presented for payment Rs. 500, interest collected by bank Rs. 400 and deposit by a customer directly into his bank Rs. 250. Bank reconciliation statement will show balance of ___ as per passbook.
A. Rs. 4,150
B. Rs. 4,000
C. Rs. 4,500
D. None of the above

Q.23 A company cannot issue:
A. Redeemable Equity Shares
B. Redeemable Preference Shares
C. Redeemable Debentures
D. Fully Convertible Debentures

Q.24 Preference shareholders are _________ of the company.
A. Creditors
B. Owners
C. Customers
D. Borrowers

Q.25 A Cheque received and paid into the bank on the same day is recorded in the _________.
A. Cash column of the cash book
B. Bank column of the cash book
C. Both the cash and bank columns of the book
D. The credit balance as per pass book

Q.26 Providing a _______ is the bank's way of keeping the customers informed of the entries made in their accounts.
A. Bank passbook
B. Bank statement
C. Cheque book
D. Either (A) or (B)

Q.27 The money deposited with bank is ______ to bank account while money withdrawn from the bank is ______ to bank account.
A. Debited, Credited
B. Credited, Debited
C. Debited, Debited
D. Credited, Credited

Q.28 A bank account is a personal account and the account-holders record their transaction with the bank in a similar manner as they do with any other person.
A. True
B. False, because bank account is a real account.
C. False, because account holders record their transaction with the bank in a similar manner as a nominal account.
D. Both (B) and (C)

Q.29 If you start with cash book favourable balance in Bank Reconciliation Statement, which item will be added?
A. Cheque deposited but not credited by the bank
B. Cheque omitted to be deposited in the bank
C. Any amount directly collected by the bank on behalf of customer but not recorded in cash book
D. Overcast debit side of cash book

Q.30 Credit balance as per cash book means
A. Surplus cash
B. Bank overdraft
C. Term deposits with bank
D. None of these

Q.31 Insurance & Freight on machinery purchased is_________.
A. Capital Expenditure
B. Deferred Revenue Expenditure
C. Revenue Expenditure
D. Prepaid Expenses

Q.32 The ideal quick ratio is
A. 1 : 2
B. 1 : 1
C. 5 : 1
D. None of the above

Q.33 _______ is the indicator of long term solvency position of an enterprise.
A. Acid Test Ratio
B. Quick Ratio
C. Current Ratio
D. Debt Equity Ratio

Q.34 _______ ratio is also known fixed charges cover for interest as well as principal amount.
A. Debt service coverage
B. Capital gearing
C. Market test
D. Earning per share

Q.35 _______ is the ratio of total current assets to total current liabilities.
A. Current Ratio
B. Liquid Ratio
C. Debt Equity Ratio
D. Proprietary Ratio

Q.36 A _______ ratio is an indicator of overtrading of total assets, and a _______ ratio reveals idle capacity.

A. low, low   **B.** low, high

C. high, low   **D.** high, high

Q.37 Return on Shareholder's Funds =

A. $\frac{Net\ Profit\ after\ interest\ and\ Tax}{Shareholder's\ Funds} + 100$

B. $\frac{Net\ Profit\ after\ interest\ and\ Tax}{Shareholder's\ Funds} - 100$

C. $\frac{Net\ Profit\ after\ interest\ and\ Tax}{Shareholder's\ Funds} \times 100$

D. $\frac{Net\ Profit\ after\ interest\ and\ Tax}{Shareholder's\ Funds} \div 100$

Q.38 _______ ratio is also known as overall profitability ratio or return on capital employed.

A. Profitability

B. Return on Investment

C. Return on Shareholder's Funds

D. Return on Assets

Q.39 _______ give some yardstick to measure the profit in relative terms with reference to sales, assets or capital employed.

A. Profitability ratios   **B.** Turnover ratios

C. Financial ratios   **D.** Market test ratios

Q.40 _______ is/are interested in the operational efficiency, earning capacities and financial health of the business.

A. Management   **B.** Shareholders

C. Investors   **D.** Creditors

Q.41 Ratio analysis focuses on

A. liability   **B.** profitability

C. solvency   **D.** All of the above

Q.42 Nominal Share Capital is

A. That part of authorised capital which is issued by the company.

B. The amount of capital which is actually applied by the prospective shareholders.

C. The amount of capital which is actually paid by the shareholders.

D. The maximum amount of share capital which a company is authorised to issue.

Q.43 Which among the following statements is not correct?

A. In India, the accounting standards are issued by Accounting Standards Board under ICAI.

B. Compliance with accounting standards is the duty of Auditor.

C. Single entry system is a scientific method of accounting.

D. Accounting standard 6 relates to depreciation accounting.

Q.44 Interest accrued but not due means

A. Interest not paid as company defaulted in payment of interest.

B. Interest not paid as the due date did not arrive.

C. Interest paid and received by the debenture holders

D. All of the above

Q.45 Dividend paid before the end of the financial year is known as

A. Interim dividend   **B.** Unclaimed dividend

C. Proposed dividend   **D.** None of the above

Q.46 D Ltd. issued 1,00,000 equity shares of Rs 10 each at a premium of Rs. 2 per share. The amount payable was Rs. 2 on application, Rs. 5 on allotment (including premium) & rest on first & final call. Applications were received for 1,20,000 shares. Excess application money was refunded to applications. All monies due were received except the allotment and first & final call monies on 1,000 shares. These shares were forfeited and reissued at Rs 9 per share.

Amount to be refunded on allotment for excess application will be _____.

A. Rs. 2,50,000   **B.** Rs. 2,35,000

C. Rs. 30,000   **D.** Rs. 40,000

Q.47 The premium on issue of shares must be treated as

A. Cost of capital   **B.** Capital receipt

C. Revenue receipt   **D.** Capital expense

Q.48 _______ refers to that part of subscribed capital which has actually been paid by the shareholder to whom shares has been allotted.

A. Paid-up capital

B. Subscribed capital

C. Issued capital

D. Nominal or authorized capital

Q.49 _______ is stated in the Memorandum of Association as the share capital of the company.

A. Called-up capital   **B.** Paid-up capital

C. Authorized capital   **D.** Subscribed capital

Q.50 Capital Reserve comes under

A. Part of uncalled capital

B. Reserve and surplus

C. Accumulated profits

D. Reserve capital

Q.51 Premium on issue of shares is shown under the head

A. Shareholder Fund

B. Non-Current Liabilities

C. Current Liabilities

D. None of the above

Q.52 The amount of calls in arrears is reduced from _______ to arrive at _______.

A. Issued capital: Called-up capital

B. Called-up capital: Issued capital

C. Paid-up capital; Called-up capital

D. Called-up capital; Paid-up capital

Q.53 There must be at least _______ gap between two calls.

A. One month   **B.** Two month

C. Three month   **D.** Four month

Q.54 The law limits the commission payable on the issue of debentures to

A. 2%   **B.** 2½%   **C.** 3%   **D.** 5%

Q.55 Which of the following errors is an error of omission?

A. Purchase of Rs. 2,000 has been recorded in the Sales Return Book.

B. Repairs to machinery have been debited to Machinery Accounts.

C. The total of purchase journal has not been posted to the Purchase Account.

D. Legal charges paid to Mr. Lawyer have been debited to his account.

Q.56 While checking the accounts of ABC, the following discrepancies were noticed, even though the Trial Balance was made to balance by putting the difference to Suspense Account.

(i) Sales day book for the month of June 2012 was found overcast by Rs. 7,000.

(ii) A credit purchase of Rs. 3,000 was omitted to be recorded in the days book.

(iii) Rs. 4,300 received from A credited to A's account as Rs. 3,400.

(iv) Purchase of Office Equipment worth Rs. 5,000 included in trading purchases.

From the above details, what would have been the difference in Trial Balance which was made to balance by opening Suspense Account?

A. Debit side short by Rs. 9,100

B. Credit side short by Rs. 9,100

C. Debit side more by Rs. 7,900

D. Credit side more by Rs. 6,100

Q.57 Which of the following errors is an error of principle?

A. Total sales figure was taken as Rs. 19,373 instead of Rs. 19,733.

B. A discount of Rs. 30 avowed to Mr. A was not recorded in the discount allowed account.

C. Legal charges for acquisition of building for Rs. 500 were entered in the Legal Expenses Account.

D. Rs. 1,000 received from Mr. X was posted to the credit of Mr. M.

Q.58 Balances of accounts are transferred to

A. Trial Balance

B. Trading Account

C. Profit and Loss Account

D. Balance Sheet

Q.59 To whom is the term "insider trading" related?

A. Hawala   **B.** Public

C. Share market   **D.** Tax

Q.60 Which of the following is not a process in the preparation of a trial balance?

A. Recording   **B.** Summarizing

C. Classifying   **D.** Interpretation

Q.61 Which of the following will lead to understatement of net profit?

A. Amortization of fictitious assets

B. Treating capital expenditure as revenue expenditure

C. Treating revenue expenditure as capital expenditure

D. Creation of general reserve

Q.62 Capital expenditure is an expenditure which

A. Benefits the current accounting period

B. Will benefit the next accounting period

C. Will benefit the current as well as future accounting periods

D. Results in the acquisition of a current asset

Q.63 Legal expenses incurred in defending a suit for breach of contract to supply goods come under

A. Revenue expenditure

B. Capital expenditure

C. Deferred revenue expenditure

D. None of the above

Q.64 Ram and Shyam were friends and in need of funds. On 1.1.2006, Ram drew a bill for Rs. 2,00,000 for six months on Shyam. On 4.1.2006, Ram got the bill discounted at 10% p.a. and remitted 40% of the proceeds to Shyam. The cheque sent to Shyam is for

A. Rs. 80,000   **B.** Rs. 72,000

C. Rs. 76,000   **D.** Rs. 70,000

Q.65 The portion of the capital which can be called-up only on the winding up of the Company is called (CPT Dec. 2012)

A. Authorised Capital   **B.** Called up Capital

C. Uncalled Capital   **D.** Reserve Capital

Q.66 'A' has discounted 3 months bill @ 10% p.a. from bank and given credit of 11,700. On due date, the bill was dishonoured and noting charges of Rs.50 was paid by bank. The amount by which A's A/c will be debited by bank is________

A. 13,050   **B.** 11,050   **C.** 12,050   **D.** 12,250

Q.67 Dishonour of cheque is recorded in

A. Double/Triple column cash book

B. Sales book

C. Purchases book

D. Bills receivable book

Q.68 Bills receivable account is a

A. Nominal account   **B.** Personal account

C. Real account   **D.** None of the above

Q.69 The Acceptor of Bills of Exchange is the

A. Debtor   **B.** Creditor

C. Seller   **D.** None of the above

Q.70 Drawee means a person who

A. Makes the order

B. Accepts the bill

C. Takes the payment on the due date

D. Is the creditor

Q.71 Which of these is not an essential feature of a bill of exchange?

A. Unconditional

B. In writing

C. Certainty of amount

D. Amount to be paid in foreign currency

Q.72 When bill discounted with the bank is dishonoured,

A. Acceptor's account is debited in the books of drawer

B. Bills receivable account is credited in the books of drawer

C. The bank account is debited in the books of drawer

D. Bills payable account is debited in the books of drawer

Q.73 A had a capital of Rs. 75,000. He also had goods amounting to Rs. 15,000 which he had purchased on credit and the payment had not been made. The value of the total assets of the business is

A. Rs. 90,000

B. Rs. 60,000

C. Rs. 75,000

D. Cannot be calculated

Q.74 Given information:

Capital at the end= Rs.7,000

Capital introduced = Rs.5,000

Drawings= Rs.8,000

Loss= Rs.10,000

With the above information, capital in the beginning is equal to

_________.

A. Rs. 65,000   **B.** Rs. 1,15,000

C. Rs. 20,000   **D.** Rs. 9,000

Q.75 The amount spent in order to produce and sell the goods and services which produce the revenue is called

A. Revenue   **B.** Expense

C. Assets   **D.** Investment

Q.76 Depreciating fixed assets over their useful life is an example of which of the following concepts/conventions?

A. Money Measurement Concept

B. Going Concern Concept

C. Cost Concept

D. Matching Concept

Q.77 X Ltd. purchased goods for Rs. 5 lakh and sold $9/10^{th}$ of the value of goods for Rs. 6 lakh. Net expenses during the year were Rs. 25,000. The company reported its net profit as Rs. 75,000. Which of the following concepts is violated by the company?

A. Conservatism Concept

B. Realization

C. Matching

D. Accrual

Q.78 The underlying accounting principle(s) necessitating amortization of intangible asset(s) is/are

A. Cost Concept   **B.** Realization Concept

C. Matching Concept   **D.** Both (A) and (C)

Q.79 The basic concept(s) related to Profit and Loss Account is/are

A. Realization Concept   **B.** Matching Concept

C. Cost Concept   **D.** Both (A) and (B)

Q.80 Personal Account shows the credit balance of

A. Cash in hand

B. The amount payable

C. Income

D. The amount receivable

Q.81 Personal accounts can take the form of

A. Natural person accounts like proprietor's account, suppliers account, receivers account (like Mohan's a/c, Shashi's A/c, Naresh's a/c), etc.

B. Artificial persons' and body of persons' accounts like limited company's account, bank account, insurance company's account any governments account, etc.

C. Representative personal accounts like salaries outstanding accounts, unexpired insurance account, interest received in advance account, etc.

D. All of the above

Q.82 Which of the following is related to nominal account?

A. Bank account

B. Commission account

C. Furniture account

D. Interest received in advance account

Q.83 Authorised Capital of a Company is mentioned in :

A. Memorandum of Association

B. Articles of Association

C. Prospectus

D. Statement in lieu of Prospectus

Q.84 Which of these is not a special purpose journal?

A. Cash journal   **B.** Purchase journal

C. Debtors journal   **D.** Sales journal

Q.85 Cheques received but deposited on the next day are recorded in

A. Cash column of cash book

B. Bank column of cash book

C. Both (1) and (2)

D. None of the above

Q.86 Which of these transactions will not be recorded in cash book?

A. Cash received from debtors

B. Cash paid to creditors

C. Salary remained outstanding

D. Cash deposited with bank

Q.87 Which of the following is a liability of a firm?

A. Debit balance of analytical Petty Cash Book

B. Credit balance of Bank Pass book

C. Debit balance of Bank column of Cash Book

D. Credit balance of Bank column of Cash Book

Q.88 A & B enter into a joint venture by opening a joint bank account contributing Rs10,00,000. The profit sharing ratio between A and B is 3:2. How much amount to be contributed by A?

A. Rs 6, 00, 000   **B.** Rs 4, 00, 000

C. Rs 3, 00, 000   **D.** Rs 5, 00, 000   Rs5,00,000

Q.89 Goods costing Rs.10,000 taken by the proprietor for personal use were credited to sales account while passing rectifying entry :

A. Drawing Account to be debited and Purchases Account to be credited.

B. Sale Account to be debited and Drawing Account to be credited.

C. Sales Account to be debited and Purchases Account to be credited.

D. Sales Account to be debited and Suspense Account to be credited.

Q.90 A ______ is a price quotation to deliver the currency in future.

A. direct quote   **B.** indirect quote

C. cross rate   **D.** forward rate

Q.91 The ask-bid spread depends upon the breadth and depth of the market for that currency and the volatility of the currency.

A. True   **B.** False

C. Partly true   **D.** Partly false

Q.92 Exchange rate is the value of currency for the purpose of conversion to other currency.

A. True   **B.** False

C. Partly true   **D.** Partly false

Q.93 Market demand is ______.

A. the sum of all individual demands

B. demand at prevailing average prices

C. ability to pay the price asked

D. demand in a perfectly free market

Q.94 Forex management

A. Is part of management science

B. Refers to generation of forex

C. In the form of domestic bank notes

D. All of the above

Q.95 The objective of ________ is to ensure that approximate recognition criteria and measurement bases are applied to provision contingent liabilities and sufficient information is disclosed in the notes to the financial statements to enable users to understand their nature, timing and amount.

A. AS 27   **B.** AS 28   **C.** AS 29   **D.** AS 30

Q.96 _________ is presented by a parent (holding company) to provide financial information about the economic activities of the group as a single economic activity.

A. Profit and Loss Account

B. Consolidated Financial Statement

C. Working Capital

D. Fund-Flow Statement

Q.97 Which of the following information relating to fixed assets should be disclosed in the financial statements as per Accounting Standard-10 ?

A. Gross book value of fixed asset at the beginning of the year

B. Gross book value of fixed asset at the end of the year

C. Net book value of fixed asset at the beginning and at the end of the year

D. $(A), (B),$ and (C)

Q.98 As per AS 2, the cost of inventories should comprise

A. Costs of Purchase   **B.** Costs of Conversion

C. Both (A) and (B)   **D.** None of the above

Q.99 Accounting standards standardize diverse accounting policies with a view to

A. Eliminate the non-comparability of financial statements and thereby improving the reliability of statements

B. Provide a set of standard accounting policies, norms and disclosure requirements

C. Both (A) and (B)

D. None of the above

Q.100 Which of the following is/are the advantage(s) of Accounting Standards?

A. To eliminate or reduce variation in accounting treatments

B. To facilitate comparison of financial statements of different companies

C. To make financial statements more informative

D. All of the above

Q.101 Accounting standards are issued by

A. Central Government

B. State Government

C. Institute of Chartered Accountants of India

D. Reserve Bank of India

Q.102 GASB stands for

A. Governmental Accounting Standards Board

B. General Accounting Standards Board

C. Geographic Accounting Standards Board

D. Gift Accounting Standards Board

Q.103 X of Kolkata sends out 500 bags to Y costing each at an invoice price of each Consignor's expenses ₹ 4,000 consignee's, non-selling expenses ₹ 1,000 , selling expense ₹ 2,000. 400 bags were sold. The amount of Inventories Reserve will be

A.   **B.** Nil

C.   **D.**

Q.104 By calculating the present value of an ordinary annuity,

A. one may come to know today's value of a series of future payments

B. one may come to know the present value of the coupon payments that he will be receiving in future

C. Both (A) and (B)

D. None of the above

Q.105 ________ can be defined as a sequence of periodic payments (or receipts) regularly over a specified period of time.

A. Simple   **B.** Compound

C. Sinking fund   **D.** Annuity

Q.106 Rahul invested Rs. 70,000 in a bank at the rate of 6.5% p.a simple interest rate. He received Rs. 85,925 after the end of term. Find out the period for which sum was invested by Rahul.

A. 6.5 years   **B.** 2.5 years   **C.** 3.5 years   **D.** 4.5 years

Q.107 _______ is/are related to inter-bank transactions.
A. Money at call and short notice
B. Advances
C. Bills receivable for collection
D. Acceptance endorsements and other obligations

Q.108 The Fifth Schedule of the Constitution provides for _____.
A. Scheduled Areas
B. Scheduled Caste
C. Scheduled Tribe
D. Both (A) & (C)

Q.109 Every banking company incorporated in India is required to transfer at least _______of its profit to the reserve fund.
A. 10%   **B.** 15%   **C.** 25%   **D.** 30%

Q.110 A cheque of Rs. 6,000 is received from Mr. Sam (our tenant) on account of rent. The correct entry is

A. Cash A/c Dr 6,000 / To Rent a/c 6,000

B. Bank A/c Dr 6,000 / To Sam's A/c 6,000

C. Bank A/c Dr 6,000 / To Rent A/c 6,000

D. None of these

Q.111 Received Rs 1100 from M/s M in settlement of Rs 1250 due from him. The nature of the journal entry to be passed for this transaction is ______.
A. Simple entry
B. Compound entry
C. Complex entry
D. Contra entry

Q.112 An old furniture is sold for Rs. 5,000 to Mr. Adarsh in cash. The correct entry is

A. Adarsh's A/c Dr 5,000 / To Furniture A/c 5,000

B. Cash A/c Dr 5,000 / To Furniture A/c 5,000

C. Bank A/c Dr 5,000 / To Furniture A/c 5,000

D. None of these

Q.113 A cheque received from a debtor, Rahul, is of Rs. 9,800 in full settlement of Rs. 10,000. The correct entry is

A. Rahul's A/c Dr 10,000 / To Cash A/c 9,800 / To Discount A/c 200

B. Cash A/c Dr 10,000 / To Rahul's A/c 10,000

C. Bank A/c Dr 9800 / Discount A/c 200 / To Rahul's A/c 10,000

D. None of the above

Q.114 A sum of Rs. 25,000 is deposited in State Bank of India. The correct entry is

A. State Bank of India's A/c Dr 25,000 / To Cash A/c 25,000

B. Cash A/c Dr 25,000 / To State Bank of India's A/c 25,000

C. Vijaya Bank's A/c Dr 25,000 / To Cash A/c 25,000

D. None of these

Q.115 Depreciation charged on machinery is Rs. 40,000. The correct entry is

A. Machinery A/c Dr 40,000 / To Depreciation A/c 40,000

B. Depreciation A/c Dr 40,000 / To Machinery A/c 40,000

C. Cash A/c Dr 40,000 / To Machinery A/c 40,000

D. None of the above

Q.116 C is a new partner in a firm consisting of partners A and B. He adds Rs. 150,000 as his 1/4th share in profits. The capitals of other partners are to be adjusted on the basis of C's contribution and profit share. Find the amount to be added by A and B, if their initial capital amounts were Rs. 180,000 and Rs. 200,000, respectively.
A. Rs. 25,000 and Rs. 45,000
B. Rs. 45,000 and Rs. 25,000
C. Rs. 20,000 and Nil
D. Rs. 70,000 and Rs. 50,000

Q.117 The net profits of a business are Rs. 1,50,000, Rs. 1,75,000 and Rs. 2,75,000 in the last 3 years. These include an investment income @ 20% p.a. of Rs. 20,000 every year, but exclude the annual insurance premium payable Rs. 10,000. Goodwill is to be valued at 1½ year purchase of average profits of 3 years. Calculate the value of goodwill.
A. Rs. 2,85,000   **B.** Rs. 3,15,000
C. Rs. 2,55,000   **D.** Rs. 3,45,000

Q.118 X, Y and Z are partners sharing in the ratio 4 : 3 : 3. X retires and the new profit ratio is 3 : 7. Goodwill of the firm is valued at Rs. 20,000. What will be the journal entry?
A. Debit Z and credit X's capital by Rs. 20,000.
B. Debit Z and credit X's capital by Rs. 8,000.
C. Debit Z and credit Y's capital by Rs. 20,000.
D. Debit Z and credit Y's capital by Rs. 8,000.

Q.119 The debit balance of profit and loss account should be
A. Debited to old and new partners in the profit sharing ratio
B. Debited to new partner only
C. Credited to old partners in old profit sharing ratio
D. Debited to old partners in the old profit sharing ratio

// Smart Answer Sheet //

Correct Indicates percentage of students who answered questions correctly.

Skipped Indicates percentage of students who skipped questions.

Q.	Ans.	Correct / Skipped
1	D	48.04 % / 15.17 %
2	B	25.36 % / 27.5 %
3	D	62.14 % / 24.65 %
4	D	42.14 % / 30.72 %
5	C	60.18 % / 28.93 %
6	C	38.75 % / 27.32 %
7	A	20.0 % / 28.93 %
8	A	17.32 % / 28.39 %
9	A	9.82 % / 32.32 %
10	C	31.79 % / 27.67 %
11	C	21.07 % / 28.22 %
12	B	28.04 % / 31.42 %
13	A	17.86 % / 23.21 %
14	C	29.11 % / 29.82 %
15	C	27.86 % / 25.89 %
16	D	57.14 % / 25.36 %

Q.	Ans.	Correct / Skipped
17	D	49.64 % / 30.54 %
18	C	21.25 % / 28.75 %
19	D	55.54 % / 8.75 %
20	A	58.21 % / 23.04 %
21	C	42.5 % / 22.14 %
22	A	38.75 % / 29.11 %
23	B	24.82 % / 16.25 %
24	B	31.07 % / 29.11 %
25	B	13.21 % / 29.83 %
26	D	57.5 % / 28.57 %
27	A	35.18 % / 20.53 %
28	A	27.5 % / 30.71 %
29	C	42.5 % / 21.96 %
30	B	37.68 % / 27.32 %
31	A	30.0 % / 25.71 %
32	B	43.75 % / 24.64 %

Q.	Ans.	Correct / Skipped
33	D	59.11 % / 18.39 %
34	A	34.64 % / 28.57 %
35	A	53.75 % / 24.46 %
36	C	40.54 % / 26.07 %
37	C	49.11 % / 30.89 %
38	B	32.5 % / 27.68 %
39	A	28.21 % / 30.18 %
40	C	28.21 % / 29.29 %
41	D	66.07 % / 21.07 %
42	A	15.18 % / 29.82 %
43	C	50.0 % / 25.36 %
44	B	32.14 % / 30.18 %
45	A	54.46 % / 22.15 %
46	D	13.04 % / 31.96 %
47	B	27.86 % / 25.89 %
48	A	31.61 % / 30.35 %

Q.	Ans.	Correct / Skipped
49	C	39.29 % / 30.35 %
50	B	45.0 % / 27.68 %
51	A	35.18 % / 25.18 %
52	D	22.5 % / 23.57 %
53	A	37.86 % / 30.35 %
54	B	23.93 % / 27.68 %
55	C	46.43 % / 25.89 %
56	D	7.68 % / 31.96 %
57	C	32.86 % / 30.0 %
58	A	24.11 % / 27.32 %
59	C	35.0 % / 25.0 %
60	D	56.96 % / 23.4 %
61	B	24.64 % / 30.9 %
62	C	46.07 % / 27.86 %
63	A	26.96 % / 25.54 %
64	C	14.82 % / 31.25 %

Q.	Ans.	Correct / Skipped
65	A	15.0 % / 29.82 %
66	C	27.5 % / 28.75 %
67	A	33.21 % / 29.11 %
68	B	16.79 % / 29.46 %
69	A	27.14 % / 29.47 %
70	B	36.07 % / 29.11 %
71	D	55.89 % / 17.86 %
72	A	11.79 % / 24.82 %
73	A	28.04 % / 30.53 %
74	C	43.75 % / 28.75 %
75	B	20.54 % / 29.46 %
76	D	12.5 % / 26.79 %
77	C	16.07 % / 31.07 %
78	C	7.32 % / 28.75 %
79	D	55.71 % / 19.47 %
80	B	23.04 % / 25.17 %

Q.	Ans.	Correct / Skipped	Q.	Ans.	Correct / Skipped	Q.	Ans.	Correct / Skipped	Q.	Ans.	Correct / Skipped	Q.	Ans.	Correct / Skipped
81	D	52.32 % / 21.25 %	89	C	17.68 % / 31.61 %	97	D	45.36 % / 31.07 %	105	D	46.96 % / 29.29 %	113	B	56.79 % / 20.89 %
82	B	28.93 % / 27.5 %	90	D	48.39 % / 28.93 %	98	C	50.18 % / 28.21 %	106	C	43.93 % / 30.53 %	114	C	36.96 % / 30.0 %
83	A	31.96 % / 29.47 %	91	A	45.0 % / 30.18 %	99	C	61.07 % / 25.72 %	107	C	17.86 % / 25.89 %	115	A	32.5 % / 26.43 %
84	C	40.54 % / 27.14 %	92	A	56.79 % / 29.46 %	100	D	63.39 % / 25.54 %	108	A	25.18 % / 29.64 %	116	B	33.39 % / 30.0 %
85	A	11.61 % / 29.82 %	93	A	28.75 % / 21.07 %	101	C	59.11 % / 29.82 %	109	D	42.32 % / 22.32 %	117	B	32.14 % / 21.07 %
86	C	57.86 % / 28.03 %	94	D	39.46 % / 29.83 %	102	A	14.82 % / 28.93 %	110	C	26.61 % / 28.03 %	118	C	17.14 % / 31.07 %
87	D	24.11 % / 30.18 %	95	C	22.5 % / 27.5 %	103	A	13.04 % / 31.96 %	111	C	41.25 % / 19.46 %	119	B	31.43 % / 22.32 %
88	A	50.36 % / 29.46 %	96	B	48.04 % / 27.32 %	104	C	53.75 % / 27.32 %	112	B	24.64 % / 29.47 %	120	C	17.86 % / 23.75 %

Performance Analysis

Avg. Score (%)	32.0%
Toppers Score (%)	99.0%
Your Score	

//Hints and Solutions//

1. An automated teller machine (ATM) is an electronic banking outlet that allows customers to complete basic transactions without the aid of a branch representative or teller. ATMs are known in different parts of the world as automated bank machines (ABM) or cash machines.

ATMs are capable of-

(i) Accepting cash/cheque

(ii) Disbursing cash

(iii) Making inter-bank transfer
Hence, the correct option is (D)

2. A data file is a computer file which stores data to be used by a computer application or system, including input and output data. A data file usually does not contain instructions or code to be executed (that is, a computer program). Most computer programs work with data files.
Hence, the correct option is (B)

3. A multi-user operating system is an operating system that allows multiple users to connect and operate a single operating system. It connects several computers through LAN or WAN. The users interact with it through terminals or computers that gave them access to the system through a network or machines such as printers, each user can handle a particular segment of a system. The operating system should have to meet the requirements of all its users in a balanced way so that if any problem would arise with one user, it does not affect any other user in the chain.

Hence, the correct option is (D)

4. Core banking is a banking service provided by a group of networked bank branches where customers may access their bank account and perform basic transactions from any of the member branch offices.

Core bank component includes-

(i) financial institution infrastructure

(ii) product build

(iii) customers management and customers overview

(iv) account administration

(v) payments

(vi) management information
Hence, the correct option is (D)

5. The concept of automated banking through Automated Teller machines (ATMs) is the result of-

(i) computersiation

(ii) technological innovation

Note- An automated teller machine (ATM) is an electronic banking outlet that allows customers to complete basic transactions without the aid of a branch representative or teller. Anyone with a credit card or debit card can access cash at most ATMs.
Hence, the correct option is (C)

6. A data file is a computer file which stores data to be used by a computer application or system, including input and output data. A data file usually does not contain instructions or code to be executed (that is, a computer program). Most computer programs work with data files.
Hence, the correct option is (C)

7. Analog computers are mostly used in scientific and mechanical fields and they provide data in a continuous form. An analog computer or analogue computer is a type of computer that uses the continuously changeable aspects of physical phenomena such as electrical, mechanical, or hydraulic quantities to model the problem being solved.

Hence, the correct option is (A)

8. The purpose of accounting is to accumulate and report on financial information about the performance, financial position, and cash flows of a business. This information is then used to reach decisions about how to manage the business, or invest in it, or lend money to it.

Hence, the correct option is (A)

9. Debtors=55,200-200=55,000.

Provision for PBDD=55,000×5%=2750.

Debtors=55,000-2,750=52,250

Discount =2% ×52,250=1,045

Hence, the correct option is (A)

10. A company limited by shares can issue only two types of shares, namely (a) equity shares, and (b) preference shares.

(a). Preference shares are those shares that enjoy preferential rights both with respect to dividends and with respect to repayment of capital either during the lifetime or on winding up of the company.

(b). Equity shares are long-term financing sources for any company. These shares are issued to the general public and are non-redeemable in nature. Investors in such shares hold the right to vote, share profits and claim assets of a company.

Hence, the correct option is (C).

11. AS 13 deals with accounting for investments.

AS 13 Accounting for Investments is widely used and deals with accounting for investments in financial statements prepared by a company and prescribes various disclosure requirements. AS 13 Investments are assets held by an enterprise for earning income by way of dividends, interests and rentals, for Capital appreciation, or for other benefits to the investing enterprise. Assets held as stock-in-trade are not 'Investments'.

Hence, the correct option is (C).

12. Assets = Advance tax + sundry assets, i.e. Rs. 5,25,000. The same are the liabilities which include Capital + Profit + Provision + Liabilities.
Hence, the correct option is (B)

13. Opening stock Rs. 4,000 + Purchase Rs. 36,000 - Cost of goods sold Rs. 28,000 (35,000 - 20%)

Thus, stock left Rs. 12,000, out of which 50% stock is obsolete and valued at 50%, i.e. Rs. 3,000.

This stock along with other goods of Rs. 6,000 will amount to Rs. 9,000.
Hence, the correct option is (A)

14. Profit is 20% of sales, i.e. if sales Rs. 100, profit will be Rs. 20 and thus, cost will be Rs. 80.

Thus, profit on cost will be 20/80 x 100, i.e. 25%.
Hence, the correct option is (C)

15. Out of total sales, normal goods sold are Rs. 10,00,000 where the profit is 20% of cost and thus, 1/6 of sales, i.e. Rs. 1,66,667 but there is loss in damage goods of Rs. 10,000.

Thus, net profit = Rs. 1,56,667.
Hence, the correct option is (C)

16. Sensitivity analysis for NPV determination identifies-

(i) areas of concern in an investment opportunity.

(ii) those factors which are sensitive to the profitability of the investment opportunity.

(iii) those areas where more efforts are required to be made to explore more information.

Note- In corporate finance, sensitivity analysis refers to an analysis of how sensitive the result of a capital budgeting technique is to a variable, say discount rate, while keeping other variables constant. Sensitivity analysis is useful because it tells the model user how dependent the output value is on each input.
Hence, the correct option is (D)

17. The advantages of NPV and IRR methods are-

(i) They take into account time value of money.

(ii) They focus on cash flows rather than on accounting profits.

Note- The NPV method results in a dollar value that a project will produce, while IRR generates the percentage return that the project is expected to create. The NPV method focuses on project surpluses, while IRR is focused on the breakeven cash flow level of a project.
Hence, the correct option is (D)

18. The internal rate of return is a metric used in financial analysis to estimate the profitability of potential investments. The internal rate of return is a discount rate that makes the net present value (NPV) of all cash flows equal to zero in a discounted cash flow analysis.
Hence, the correct option is (C)

19. The time value of money (TVM) is the concept that money you have now is worth more than the identical sum in the future due to its potential earning capacity. This core principle of finance holds that provided money can earn interest, any amount of money is worth more the sooner it is received.
Hence, the correct option is (D)

20. Pay-back period = 20,000/4,000=5 years.

Note- The payback period refers to the amount of time it takes to recover the cost of an investment. Simply put, the payback period is the length of time an investment reaches a break-even point.
Hence, the correct option is (A)

21. Given -

Face Value = Rs. 5,000

Interest rate = 12%

Interest earned is Rs. 600 (5000 x 12%).

Thus, current yield = 600/4500 x 100 = 13.3%

Hence, the correct option is (C)

22. Balance is required as per passbook. Thus, all of the above transactions have to be added because bank has credited interest, collected money from customer and has not debited the cheque issued yet.

3,000 + 500 + 400 + 250 = Rs. 4,150
Hence, the correct option is (A)

23. A company cannot issue redeemable preference shares for a period exceeding 20 years. A company may issue preference shares which are liable to be redeemed within a period not exceeding twenty years from the date of their issue under section 55 of the Companies Act 2013

Hence,the correct option is (B).

24. Like the ordinary or equity shareholders, preference shareholders are also owners of the company. The only difference is that preference shareholders have dividend rights before the equity shareholders.
Hence, the correct option is (B).

25. Cash book is having two columns i.e cash and bank column. When a cheque is received and deposited on the same day in to the bank, this will be recorded in bank column of the cash book.
Hence, the correct option is (B)

26. Bank pass book is a copy of the customer's account with the bank in the books of the bank. So it is prepared by the bank.

A bank statement is a summary of financial transactions that occurred at a certain institution during a specific time period. For example, a typical bank statement may show your deposits and withdrawals for a certain month.
Hence, the correct option is (D)

27. The money deposited with bank is debited, to bank account while money withdrawn from the bank is credited to bank account.

Note- Credited to your account means amount has been deposited to your account(this will be your income). Debited from your account means withdrawn from your account(This will be your expense).
Hence, the correct option is (A)

28. A bank account is a personal account and the account-holders record their transaction with the bank in a similar manner as they do with any other person.

Note- Bank account is an example of personal account and not nominal account. All the accounts related to an individual, a firm or a company are termed as a personal accounts.
Hence, the correct option is (A)

29. There are instances when debtors(customers) directly deposits money into firm's bank account. But, the firm does not receive the intimation from any source till it receives the bank statement. In this case, the bank records the receipts in the firm's account at the bank but the same is not recorded in the firm's cash book. As a result, the balance shown in the bank passbook will be more than the balance shown in the firm's cash book.
Hence, the correct option is (C)

30. A credit balance in cash book is an overdraft as per passbook. The bank maintains the customer account which is further printed in the passbook. The passbook is made from the viewpoint of the bank hence customer depositing money is a liability to the bank and is credited. Therefore when the balance is unfavourable it shows a debit balance because they will receive money from the customer. The debits and credit of passbook and cash book are opposite.

Hence, the correct option is (B)

31. Insurance & Freight on machinery purchased is Capital Expenditure.

Capital expenditure refers to funds that are used by a company to acquire, improve or maintain long term assets to improve the efficiency or earning capacity of the company. Capital Expenditures are for fixed assets, which are expected to be productive assets for a long period of time. All the amount paid up to the point an asset is ready for use is included in the cost of that asset.

Hence, the correct option is (A).

32. Generally, the acid test ratio should be 1:1 or higher; however, this varies widely by industry. In general, the higher the ratio, the greater the company's liquidity (i.e., the better able to meet current obligations using liquid assets).
Hence, the correct option is (B)

33. Long term solvency is measured by Debt Equity Ratio.

Note-The debt-to-equity ratio is a financial ratio indicating the relative proportion of shareholders' equity and debt used to finance a company's assets. Closely related to leveraging, the ratio is also known as risk, gearing or leverage.
Hence, the correct option is (D)

34. In corporate finance, the debt-service coverage ratio (DSCR) is a measurement of the cash flow available to pay current debt obligations. The ratio states net operating income as a multiple of debt obligations due within one year, including interest, principal, sinking-fund and lease payments.
Hence, the correct option is (A)

35. Current Ratio is the ratio of total current assets to total current liabilities.
Current ratio is a comparison of current assets to current liabilities, calculated by dividing your current assets by your current liabilities. Potential creditors use the current ratio to measure a company's liquidity or ability to pay off short-term debts.
Hence, the correct option is (A)

36. A high ratio is an indicator of over-trading of total assets while a low ratio reveals idle capacity. The traditional standard for the ratio is two times. Stock Turnover Ratio: It denotes the speed at which the inventory will be converted into sales, thereby contributing for the profits of the concern.
Hence, the correct option is (C)

37. $\dfrac{Net\ Profit\ after\ interest\ and\ Tax}{Shareholder\text{'}s\ Funds} \times 100$

Note- Return on Shareholders' Funds is one of the ratios of overall profitability group, which indicates the profitability of a firm in relation to the funds supplied by the shareholders or owners. This ratio is very important from the owner's point of view as it helps the firm to know whether the firm has earned enough returns to repay its shareholders or not.
Hence, the correct option is (C)

38. Return on investment is a ratio between net profit and cost of investment. A high ROI means the investment's gains compare favourably to its cost. As a performance measure, ROI is used to evaluate the efficiency of an investment or to compare the efficiencies of several different investments.
Hence, the correct option is (B)

39. Profitability ratios are a class of financial metrics that are used to assess a business's ability to generate earnings relative to its revenue, operating costs, balance sheet assets, or shareholders' equity over time, using data from a specific point in time.

1. Profitability ratios are metrics that assess a company's ability to generate income relative to its revenue, operating costs, balance sheet assets, or shareholders' equity.**2.** Profitability ratios show how efficiently a company generates profit and value for shareholders.**3.** Higher ratio results are often more favourable, but ratios provide much more information when compared to results of similar companies, the company's own historical performance, or the industry average.
Hence, the correct option is (A)

40. Investors is/are interested in the operational efficiency, earning capacities and financial health of the business.

Note- Shareholders are interested in financial statement analysis to know the profitability of the organization. Profitability shows the growth potentiality of an organization and safety of investment of shareholders. Investors and lenders are interested to know the solvency position of an organization.
Hence, the correct option is (C)

41. Ratio Analysis- The ratios are used to identify trends over time for one company or to compare two or more companies at one point in time. Financial statement ratio analysis focuses on three key aspects of a business: liquidity, profitability, and solvency.
Hence, the correct option is (D)

42. The authorised capital of a company (sometimes referred to as the authorised share capital, registered capital or nominal capital, particularly in the United States) is the maximum amount of share capital that the company is authorised by its constitutional documents to issue (allocate) to shareholders.

Hence, the correct option is (A).

43. Single entry system of accounts do not record two-fold aspects of each and every transactions, hence, it is not a scientific system of keeping accounting records. Preparation of a trial balance is not possible, because the method of double entry system is not followed for each business transaction.
Hence, the correct option is (C)

44. In one word interest accrued but not due means Interest amount computed as per the period of computation but the payment of amount of installment time is still available.
Hence, the correct option is (B)

45. An interim dividend is a dividend payment made before a company's annual general meeting (AGM) and the release of final financial statements. This declared dividend usually accompanies the company's interim financial statements.
Hence, the correct option is (A)

46. The amount received on shares issued is Rs 12,00,000. The application money is Rs 2 per share and application received is 1,20,000 then application money received is Rs 2,40,000. But application issued were still 100000 as it is case of over-subscription and hence application money received on issuance of share is Rs 2,00,000. There amount to refunded is Rs 40,000 (Rs 2,40,000-Rs 2,00,000).
Hence, the correct option is (D)

47. These have a nature of non-recurrence, besides that, they are situated in the balance sheet in the liabilities portion of them. The capital receipt is always in the interchange for the income. The capital receipt is a kind of cash-flow in the business that does not occur over and over again and this eventually, leads to the creation of liabilities in the future and also, the decrement of assets takes place in the future.

All of the capital receipts are free from taxation unless there is a provision to tax it. Various types of Gifts and loans are the types of the capital receipts that do not attract tax and are tax-free. So, in addition to non-recurring, Capital receipts are those non-routine receipts which either becomes a load and responsibility or cause a vivid depletion in the assets of the government or any organization and business.

The following sources are the generators of the capital receipt:

• Additional capital and mentioned assets introduced by the owner or the possessor

• Debentures and the other issues of debt instruments

• Loans borrowed from a bank or from a financial institution.

• Various insurance Claims.

• Issue of Shares

So, basically, capital receipts are those that are the derivation of the not so normal operations of a business. Besides that, the effect of capital receipt is depicted in the balance sheet. These receipts are not at all a part of normal operations of government business. For example, a sale of fixed assets, etc.
Hence, the correct option is (B)

48. Paid-up capital is the amount of money a company has received from shareholders in exchange for shares of stock. Paid-up capital is created when a company sells its shares on the primary market, directly to investors. When shares are bought and sold among investors on the secondary market, no additional paid-up capital is created as proceeds in those transactions go to the selling shareholders, not the issuing company.
Hence, the correct option is (A)

49. The authorised capital of a company (sometimes referred to as the authorised share capital, registered capital or nominal capital, particularly in the United States) is the maximum amount of share capital that the company is authorised by its constitutional documents to issue (allocate) to shareholders.
Hence, the correct option is (C)

50. This item comes under Liabilities side of the balance sheet under the head 'Reserves & Surplus'. In case of a company Capital Reserve arises only in one situations: when there are any unrealized profit which is to be recorded in books of accounts.
Hence, the correct option is (B)

51. Share premium is the credited difference in price between the par value, or face value, of shares, and the total price a company received for recently-issued shares. share premium account appears in the shareholders' equity section of the balance sheet.
Hence, the correct option is (A)

52. Called up Capital-

According to Section 2(15) of the Companies Act, 2013, Called up Capital is the part of the capital which the company calls for payment. This is the total amount that the company calls-up on the issued shares.

Paid Up capital-

Paid up capital is the part of called up capital actually paid or credited by shareholders on the issued shares. Mathematically, Paid up capital = Called up capital – Calls in Arrears.
Hence, the correct option is (D)

53. Second, there must be an interval of at least one month between the making of two calls unless otherwise provided by the articles of association of the company.
Hence, the correct option is (A)

54. ADVERTISEMENTS: The law limits the commission in case of issue of shares to 5% (or a lower rate if the Articles so state) of the issue price of shares and in case of issue of debentures to 2½% or such lower rate as is provided in the Articles.
Hence, the correct option is (B)

55. The total of purchase journal has not been posted to the Purchase Account. When an entry is not posted, it is an error or omission.

Note- Errors of Omission: – Error of omission is divided into two parts i.e., Complete omission of transactions and partial omission of transactions. In case of error of complete omission, a transaction is completely omitted to be recorded in the books of accounts. An accountant forgets to record such entry in the subsidiary books.

Example – omission to record goods sold to a vendor, omission to record asset purchased etc. In case of partial omission, the

transaction is recorded at the debit side and omitted to be recorded at the corresponding credit side. Partial omissions affect only one account. For Example – Goods purchased from Mr X, recorded in purchase book but no entry made in Mr X's account.
Hence, the correct option is (C)

56. Correct Answer:

(i)   Sales credited more by Rs. 7,000

(ii) No suspense account

(iii) A's account under credited by Rs. 900

(iv) No suspense account.

Thus, credit side is more by Rs. 6,100.
Hence, the correct option is (D)

57. The correct answer is "Legal charges for acquisition of building for Rs. 500 were entered in the Legal Expenses Account".

Note- When a revenue item is shown as capital item and vice versa, it is error of principle. An error of principle is an accounting mistake in which an entry violates a fundamental principle of accounting or a fundamental accounting principle established by a company.
Hence, the correct option is (C)

58. Balances of accounts are transferred to Trial Balance.

Note- The trial balance period is the time between final posting to the ledger and transfer of account balances to financial statements. And, they also to search for errors that the trial balance overlooks.

Hence, the correct option is (A)

59. The term insider trading is associated with the share market.

Insider trading is the buying or selling of a publicly traded company's stock by someone who has non-public, material information about that stock.

Hence, the correct option is (C)

60. Interpretation is analysis after final accounts are prepared.

Note- A trial balance is a bookkeeping worksheet in which the balance of all ledgers are compiled into debit and credit account column totals that are equal. A company prepares a trial balance periodically, usually at the end of every reporting period.
Hence, the correct option is (D)

61. Treating capital expenditure as revenue expenditure will lead to more expenditures and thus, profits would be understated.

Note- When we treated Capital Expenditure as revenue expenditure, then the Balance of Income Statement is understated in the current year but the net income shown in the Income Statement in the next accounting year will be overstated as we do not charge any Depreciation On Non- Current Assets.
Hence, the correct option is (B)

62. Capital expenditure results in benefit in more than one accounting period.

Note- Capital expenditures are expenses a company makes to sustain and expand its business over a period of years. A capital

expense is the cost of an asset that has usefulness, helping create profits for a period longer than the current tax year.
Hence, the correct option is (C)

63. A revenue expenditure is a cost that will be an expense in the accounting period when the expenditure takes place. Revenue expenditures are often discussed in the context of fixed assets. The revenue expenditures take place after a fixed asset had been put into service and simply keeps the asset in working order.

Hence, the correct option is (A)

64. Total discount of bill is 2,00,000 $\times \dfrac{6}{12} \times \dfrac{10}{100}$ = Rs. 10,000.

40% of discount will be Rs. 4,000.

Thus, out of 40% amount due, i.e. Rs. 80,000,

Rs. 4,000 will be subtracted.

Correct Answer: Rs. 76,000
Hence, the correct option is (C)

65. According to Section 2(8) of the Companies Act, 2013 'authorised capital' means Such capital as is authorised by the memorandum of a company to be the maximum amount of share capital of a company. Ans. Part of capital of a company which is called-up only on winding up is called 'reserve capital'.

Hence, the correct option is (A).

66. Let the actual amount of bill be Rs. x.

Discount @ 10% p.a. for 3 months will be $\dfrac{x}{40}$ and net amount realised will be x - $\dfrac{x}{40} = \dfrac{39}{40}$.

Now, $\dfrac{39}{40}$ of x = 11,700

Thus, the amount of bill is Rs. 12,000, but on maturity being dishonoured, it will be debited along with charges of Rs. 50. Thus, the correct answer will be Rs. 12,050.

67. The dishonour of cheques is recorded on the payment side or credit side of the bank column of cash book. When a cheque is dishonoured, the Bank A/c is credited and, thus, it is credited in the bank column of the cash book.
Hence, the correct option is (A)

68. In belts of exchange when a Debtor accepts the bill drawn against him, the debtor converts into bills receivable for business. the business will now get money in exchange of bills receivable. so bills receivable considered as an assets to business. bills receivable is a personal account.
Hence, the correct option is (B)

69. A debtor is an entity that owes a debt to another entity. The entity may be an individual, a firm, a government, a company or other legal person. The counterparty is called a creditor. When the counterpart of this debt arrangement is a bank, the debtor is more often referred to as a borrower.
Hence, the correct option is (A)

70. A person who accepts the bill is called Acceptor. The person on whom the bill is drawn is called drawee. Bill needs to be signed(accepted) by the drawee, Therefore when drawee accepts

the Bill and also becomes the acceptor.
Hence, the correct option is (B)

71. The following are the features of bills of exchange:

- A bill of exchange an instrument in writing.
- It is drawn and signed by the maker i.e. drawer of the bill.
- It is drawn on a specific person i.e. drawee, to pay the specified amount.
- Contains an unconditional order to a person i.e. drawee.
- To make an instrument of value the drawee must accept it.
- The specified amount is payable to the person whose name is mentioned in the bill or to his order or to the bearer.
- It specifies the date by which amount should be paid.
- Payment of the bill must be in the legal currency of the country.
- It must be properly stamped.
- It must bear a revenue stamp.

Hence, the correct option is (D)

72. Acceptor's account is debited in the books of drawer
Logic : Bank has account of Drawer and it has money. Bank will deduct same money from his account and debit of his account because bill dishonoured.

Hence, the correct option is (A)

73. Capital
Goods purchased on credit .
Now, to get the value of the total assets of the business we add the capital and the goods purchased on credit:

Total Assets $= 75,000 + 15,000$

Total Assets $= 90,000$

Thus, the value of the total assets of the business is .
Hence, the correct option is (A)

74. Solution to the given problem can be given through the below equation:

Opening Capital + Capital Introduced + Profit - Drawings = Closing Capital

By putting the information:

Opening Capital + Rs.5000 - Rs.10000 (Loss) - Rs.8000 = Rs.7000

Opening Capital - Rs.13000 = Rs.7000

Opening Capital = Rs.7000 + Rs.13000

Opening Capital = Rs.20000

Hence, the correct option is (C)

75. The amount spent in order to produce and sell the goods and services which produce the revenue is called Expense.

Note- The cost which business incurs for producing goods and services or for using services is called expenses. These include

payments made for wages, salaries, freight, advertisement, rent, insurance etc. In other words, we can say that the cost of earning revenue is an expense.
Hence, the correct option is (B)

76. The matching concept is an accounting practice whereby firms recognize revenues and their related expenses in the same accounting period. Firms report "revenues," that is, along with the "expenses" that brought them. The purpose of the matching concept is to avoid misstating earnings for a period.
Hence, the correct option is (D)

77. Matching concept requires the expenses must relate to the goods and services sold during that period to arrive at the net profits of the enterprise. Hence matching concept requires the recognition of revenue and expenses on a comparable basis. In the above question that amount of as net profit was arrived at by deducting (being cost of purchases) expenses from the sale proceeds of This does not follow matching concept since the cost of goods sold is to be deducted and not the cost of purchases, since some purchases have been left in stock. So the net profit using matching concept is $6,00,000$ less cost of goods (i.e. less expenses of
Hence, the correct option is (C)

78. The matching concept is an accounting practice whereby firms recognize revenues and their related expenses in the same accounting period. Firms report "revenues," that is, along with the "expenses" that brought them. The purpose of the matching concept is to avoid misstating earnings for a period.
Hence, the correct option is (C)

79. Realization concept in accounting, also known as the revenue recognition principle, refers to the application of the accruals concept towards the recognition of revenue (income). Under this principle, revenue is recognized by the seller when it is earned irrespective of whether cash from the transaction has been received or not.

The matching concept is an accounting practise whereby firms recognize revenues and their related expenses in the same accounting period. Firms report "revenues," that is, along with the "expenses" that brought them. The purpose of the matching concept is to avoid misstating earnings for a period.
Hence, the correct option is (D)

80. Credit Balance of a Personal account indicates the amount payable.

Note- The debit balance of a personal account indicated debt owing by the person and credit balance indicates debts owing to the person concerned. For the business, the first one is account receivable or asset, while the second is accounts payable or liability
Hence, the correct option is (B)

81. Accounts recording transactions with a person or group of persons are known as personal accounts. These accounts are necessary, in particular, to record credit transactions. Personal accounts are of the following types:
1. Natural persons: An account recording transactions with an individual is termed as a natural persons' personal account. For e.g. Kamal's account, Mala's account. Both males and females are included in it.

2. Artificial persons: An account regarding financial transactions with an artificial person s created by law or otherwise is termed as an artificial persons' personal accounts. For e.g. Firms' accounts, limited companies' accounts, etc.

3. Representative personal accounts: An account indirectly representing a person pr persons is known as representative personal account. When accounts are of a similar nature and their number is large, it is better to group them under one head and open a representative personal account. For e.g. prepaid insurance, outstanding wages, etc.

Hence, the correct option is (D)

82. The entire purpose of a nominal account is to track the revenue and expenses for a company so that the net profit or net loss for a specific period can be calculated. Example of nominal accounts are service revenue, sales revenue, wage expense, utilities expense, commission, supplies expense, and interest expense.

Hence, the correct option is (B)

83. It is the maximum amount of the capital for which shares can be issued by the Company to shareholders. The Authorised capital is mentioned in the Memorandum of Association of the Company under heading of "Capital Clause". It is even decided prior to incorporation of the Company.

Hence, the correct option is (A).

84. Special journals are designed as a simple way to record the most frequently occurring transactions. There are four types of Special Journals that are frequently used by merchandising businesses: Sales journals, Cash receipts journals, Purchases journals, and Cash payments journals.

Hence, the correct option is (C)

85. It is treated as cash received on the date of receipt and recorded in the cash column on receipts side. When the cheque is deposited the entry for deposit will be passed on the day of depositing the cheque into bank.

Hence, the correct option is (A)

86. Outstanding salary is a personal representative account. As per matching concept, salary is due but not yet paid. So, Unpaid salary to be shown as liability under 'Expenses Payable' or 'Salary Payable' in Balance sheet on liabilities side and on other aspect of dual entry to be placed in Profit & Loss Account.

Hence, the correct option is (C)

87. Creditors are a liability. Creditors means the persons to whom business owes money. Creditors are the persons to whom the money is payable by the business in future. So it is a liability of business towards creditors to pay them in future so it comes under current liabilities in balance sheet.

Hence, the correct option is (D)

88. The total capital of the joint venture = Rs 10,00,000

The profit-sharing ratio between A and B = 3:2

Capital contributed by A can be calculated by profit sharing ratio

$$1000000 \times \frac{3}{5} = \text{Rs } 6,00,000$$

Hence, the correct option is (A)

89. When goods are withdrawn by the proprietor, goods are going out of the business i.e., purchases account has to credit. The journal entry for this is -

Drawings A/c   Dr 10,000
To Purchases A/c   10,000

Instead of this entry, the incorrect entry passed was -

Drawings A/c   Dr 10,000
To Sales A/c   10,000

Here, instead of purchase account sales account has been credited whereas drawings account has been rightly debited, so to cancel this entry and rectify it, sales account which was credited is to be debited to cancel the entry, and purchases account will be credited fro the original entry. Since drawings account is rightly debited, no change will be made regarding drawings account. The rectified journal entry thus becomes -

Sales A/c   Dr 10,000
To Purchases A/c   10,000

Hence, the correct option is (C)

90. A forward rate is a contracted price for a transaction that will be completed at an agreed upon date in the future. In bond markets, forward rate refers to the future yield based on interest rates and maturities.

Hence, the correct option is (D)

91. The ask-bid spread depends upon the breadth and depth of the market for that currency and the volatility of the currency.

Note- Market-makers (which you term dealers) earn the bid-ask spread by buying and selling in as short a window as possible, hopefully before the prices have moved too much.

Hence, the correct option is (A)

92. An exchange rate is the value of a country's currency vs. that of another country or economic zone. Most exchange rates are free-floating and will rise or fall based on supply and demand in the market. Some currencies are not free-floating and have restrictions.

Hence, the correct option is (A)

93. Demand is the quantity of a good or service that consumers and businesses are willing and able to buy at a given price in a given time period. Market demand is the sum of the individual demand for a product from buyers in the market.

Hence, the correct option is (A)

94. The foreign exchange market refers to the network of individuals, banks and organized financial exchanges that trade global currencies. Foreign exchange management requires its participants to enter the market to deliver and accept currencies at fluctuating exchange rates.

Hence, the correct option is (D)

95. The objective of AS 29 is to ensure that approximate recognition criteria and measurement bases are applied to provision contingent liabilities and sufficient information is disclosed in the notes to the financial statements to enable users to understand their nature, timing and amount.

Note- The objective of this Standard is to ensure that appropriate recognition criteria and measurement bases are applied to provisions and contingent liabilities and that sufficient information is disclosed in the notes to the financial statements to enable users to understand their nature, timing and amount.

The objective of this Standard is also to lay down appropriate accounting for contingent assets.
Hence, the correct option is (C)

96. Consolidated financial statements are the "financial statements of a group in which the assets, liabilities, equity, income, expenses and cash flows of the parent company and its subsidiaries are presented as those of a single economic entity", according to International Accounting Standard 27 "Consolidated and separate financial statements", and International Financial Reporting Standard 10 "Consolidated financial statements".
Hence, the correct option is (B)

97. The following information should be disclosed in the financial statements:

(i) Gross and netbook values of fixed assets at the beginning and end of an accounting period showing additions, disposals, acquisitions and other movements.

(ii) Expenditure incurred on account of fixed assets in the course of construction or acquisition. and

(iii) Revalued amounts substituted for historical costs of fixed assets, the method adopted to compute the revalued amounts, the nature of indices used, the year of any appraisal made, and whether an external valuer was involved, in case where fixed assets are stated at revalued amounts.
Hence, the correct option is (D)

98. Inventories shall be measured at the lower of cost and net realisable value.The cost of inventories shall comprise all costs of purchase, costs of conversion and other costs incurred in bringing the inventories to their present location and condition.
Hence, the correct option is (C)

99. The objective of accounting standards is to standardize the diverse accounting policies and practices with a view to eliminate to the extent possible the non-comparability of financial statements and increase relevance and reliability of financial statements.

-> eliminate the non-comparability of financial statements and thereby improving the reliability of statements.

-> provide a set of standard accounting policies, norms and disclosure requirements.

Hence, the correct option is (C)

100. An accounting standard is a common set of principles, standards, and procedures that define the basis of financial accounting policies and practices. Accounting standards apply to the full breadth of a entity's financial picture, including assets, liabilities, revenue, expenses and shareholders' equity.

The advantages of Accounting Standards are-

(i) To eliminate or reduce variation in accounting treatments.

(ii) To facilitate comparison of financial statements of different companies.

(iii) To make financial statements more informative.
Hence, the correct option is (D)

101. Indian Accounting Standard (abbreviated as Ind-AS) is the Accounting standard adopted by companies in India and issued under the supervision of Accounting Standards Board (ASB) which was constituted as a body in the year 1977. MCA has to spell out the accounting standards applicable for companies in India.
Hence, the correct option is (C)

102. Governmental Accounting Standards Board
The Government Accounting Standards Board (GASB) is a private non-governmental organization that creates accounting reporting standards, or generally accepted accounting principles (GAAP), for state and local governments in the United States.
Hence, the correct option is (A)

103. Goods sond out 500
Cost of goods 400
Profit per bags = 100
unsold goods $= 500 - 400 = 100$
∴ Inventory Reserve= 100 ✕100 =10,000
Hence, the correct option is (A)

104. By calculating the present value of an ordinary annuity-

(i) one may come to know today's value of a series of future payments.

(ii) one may come to know the present value of the coupon payments that he will be receiving in future.

Note- In contrast to the future value calculation, a present value (PV) calculation tells you how much money would be required now to produce a series of payments in the future, again assuming a set interest rate.
Hence, the correct option is (C)

105. An annuity can be defined as a sequence of periodic payments (or receipts) regularly over a specified period of time.

Note- An annuity is a series of payments made at equal intervals. Examples of annuities are regular deposits to a savings account, monthly home mortgage payments, monthly insurance payments and pension payments. Annuities can be classified by the frequency of payment dates.

Hence, the correct option is (D)

106. Solution: We know $A = P(1 + in)$
i.e. $85,925 = 70,000 \left(1 + \frac{6.5}{100} \times n\right)$
$$\frac{85,925}{70,000} = \frac{100 + 6.5n}{100}$$
$$\left(\frac{85,925}{70,000} \times 100\right) - 100 = 6.5n$$
$6.5n$=22.75 ;

n=3.5...time = 3.5 years.
Hence, the correct option is (C)

107. Money at call and short notice is related to inter-bank transactions.

Note- An item on a balance sheet of a bank. Money at Call is money that must be repaid on demand. Money at short notice may be money borrowed for, say, twenty-four hours, at a very low-interest rate. There is a great deal of money at short notice circulating in the City. When more money is offered than required, money is said to be 'easy' - when the reverse is true, money is said to be 'tight' in Lombard Street.

Hence, the correct option is (A)

108. The Fifth schedule deals with provision for the constitution of a Tribes Advisory Council. President may by order declare an area to be 'Scheduled area'.

The Sixth Schedule consists of provisions for the administration of tribal areas in Assam, Meghalaya, Tripura and Mizoram, according to Article 244 of the Indian Constitution.

Hence, the correct option is (D)

109. Under Section 17, every banking company incorporated in India is required to transfer at least 25% of its current profit to its reserve fund. It is known as statutory reserve. Only those banks get exemptions from this legal condition whose reserve along with share premium if any become equal to paid up capital.
Hence, the correct option is (C)

110. Since rent is received by cheque, we would debit bank. Rent is an income, and income is credited.

∴ Bank A/c Dr 6,000

To Rent A/c 6,000
Hence, the correct option is (C)

111. A compound journal entry is an accounting entry in which there is more than one debit, more than one credit, or more than one of both debits and credits.

Hence, it is a compound entry, as cash account and discount allowed A/c is to be debited.
Hence, the correct option is (B)

112. Cash has come in on sale of furniture, so it has to be debited. Furniture has gone out, so it has to be credited.

∴ Cash A/c Dr 5,000

To Furniture A/c 5,000
Hence, the correct option is (B)

113. Cheque is received, so we would debit bank. Discount allowed (10,000 - 9,800 = 200) is debited, since it is a loss. Rahul has paid by cheque, so he would be credited.
Hence, the correct option is (C)

114. Since cash has gone out, we have to credit it. State Bank of India is debited because we have deposited cash in it, so it has become our debtor.

∴ State Bank of India's A/c Dr 25,000

To Cash A/c 25,000
Hence, the correct option is (A)

115. Depreciation is a loss and so it would be debited. Machinery is credited, since it is a decrease in asset, and it is considered that it goes out from business.

Therefore, Depreciation A/c Dr 40,000

To Machinery A/c 40,000
Hence, the correct option is (B)

116. C's capital = Rs. 1,50,000

Thus, the capital of new firm = $1,50,000 \times \dfrac{4}{1}$ = Rs. 6,00,000

Now it is divided into a new ratio in which A and B will contribute

6,00,000 - 1,50,000= Rs. 4,50,000 equally.

Thus, they will contribute another Rs. 45,000 and Rs. 25,000, respectively.
Hence, the correct option is (B)

117. The average profits after deduction of interest and insurance premium are Rs. 1,70,000.

Thus, goodwill = 1½ x 1,70,000 = 2,55,000
Hence, the correct option is (C)

118. Y's gain = $\dfrac{3}{10} - \dfrac{3}{10} = 0$

Z's gain = $\dfrac{7}{10} - \dfrac{3}{10} = \dfrac{4}{10}$

The gaining partner is Z only and he will be debited with

$$20,000 \times \dfrac{4}{10}$$

=Rs. 8,000
Hence, the correct option is (B)

119. The P and L account should be debited to old partners in old ratio.

Note- The debit balance of a profit and loss account denoted loss. Debit balance of the profit and loss account shows that the expenses were more than the incomes.
Hence, the correct option is (C)

Q.1 Bank Reconciliation Statement is the comparison of a bank statement (sent by the bank) with the

A. cash receipt journal.
B. cash payment journal.
C. cash book.
D. financial statements.

Q.2 A cheque returned by bank marked "NSF" means that

A. bank can't verify your identity.
B. there are not sufficient funds in your account.
C. cheque has been forged.
D. cheque can't be cashed being illegal.

Q.3 Bank Reconciliation statement is prepared by

A. accountant of business.
B. manager of business.
C. controller of business.
D. accountant of the bank.

Q.4 Which one of the following methods of inventory costing yields the highest taxable income?

A. FIFO
B. LIFO
C. AVCO or averrage cost
D. Standard cost method

Q.5 Which one of the following methods of inventory costing produces ending stock costs close to the market value of the inventory?

A. FIFO
B. LIFO
C. Moving average
D. AVCO or averrage cost

Q.6 Which one of the following inventory costing methods is supposed to issue the most recently purchased goods?

A. FIFO
B. LIFO
C. AVCO or averrage cost
D. Moving average

Q.7 Opening inventory + Net purchases =

A. Ending inventory
B. Closing stock
C. Cost of goods manufactured
D. Cost of goods available for sale

Q.8 Cost of goods available for sale - closing inventory =

A. Opening inventiry
B. Cost of opening finished goods inventory
C. Work in progress ending inventory
D. Cost of goods sold

Q.9 NRV or net realizable value of inventory is the expected selling price or market value less

A. carry value of the inventory.
B. expenses necessary to complete sale.
C. cost of the stock.
D. replacement cost.

Q.10 Under which method of inventory costing, a pre-determined cost is assigned to all items of inventory?

A. Replacement cost method
B. Standard cost method
C. AVCO or average cost
D. FIFO method

Q.11 Term 'Credit' means _____ by the business.

A. receiving of benefits
B. it has no effect on business
C. providing benefits
D. it depends upon items

Q.12 When liability is reduced or decreased, it is recorded on the

A. left or credit side of the account.
B. right or debit side of the account.
C. right or credit side of the account.
D. left or debit side of the account.

Q.13 When capital is increased by an amount, it is recorded on the

A. left or credit side of the account.
B. right or debit side of the account.
C. right or credit side of the account.
D. left or debit side of the account.

Q.14 What type of expenses are paid out of Gross Profit?

A. General expenses
B. Financial expenses
C. Selling expenses
D. All of the above

Q.15 Which of the following is NOT an example of intangible assets?

A. Franchise rights
B. Goodwill
C. Patents
D. Land

Q.16 The unfavorable balance of Profit and Loss account should be

A. added to liabilities.
B. subtracted from current assets.
C. subtracted from capital.
D. subtracted from liabilities.

Q.17 Which of the following account will be credited, if business bought goods on credit from Mr. Z?

A. Purchases account
B. Mr. Z account
C. Cash account
D. Sales account

Q.18 Interest on the loan paid by business is an example of

A. revenue expense. **B.** income.

C. asset. **D.** return outward.

Q.19 Which of the following account will be credited when a typewriter is sold that has been used in the office?

A. office equipment account.

B. cash account.

C. sales account.

D. purchase account.

Q.20 The allocation of the cost of a tangible plant asset to expense in the periods, in which services are received from the asset, is termed as

A. appreciation. **B.** depreciation.

C. fluctuation. **D.** None of the above

Q.21 Which of the following item will be shown on the debit side of the debtor's account?

A. Discount received **B.** Return inwards

C. Discount allowed **D.** Credit sales

Q.22 When one or both aspects of a transaction are recorded in the wrong class or category of account, it is called

A. error of principle.

B. error of omission.

C. error of commission.

D. the error of original entry.

Q.23 Which of the following would not be considered as a component of 'cost' of stock?

A. Transportation inward costs

B. Import duties

C. Salaries of selling staff

D. Purchase price

Q.24 Which of the following is true about the treatment of insurance premium paid in advance?

A. Current asset **B.** Current liability

C. Short term liability **D.** Fixed asset

Q.25 Which of the following is (are) type(s) of Public Limited Companies?

A. Listed companies

B. Non listed companies

C. Private limited companies

D. Both listed and non listed companies

Q.26 The charter of a company that defines the limitations and powers of the company is called

A. the memorandum of association.

B. articles of association.

C. statutory report.

D. certificate of commencement.

Q.27 Merchandise on hand at either the beginning or end of the accounting period is called

A. raw material. **B.** cost of goods sold.

C. work in progress. **D.** inventory.

Q.28 In the calculation of depreciation, all of the following items are actually estimates except

A. useful life. **B.** residual value.

C. historical cost. **D.** salvage value.

Q.29 Which of the following statements is incorrect?

A. A European option can only be exercised at expiry.

B. An American option can only be exercised at the expiry.

C. A European option is a right but not an obligation.

D. An American option is a right but not an obligation.

Q.30 An agreement on a telephone or email to buy/sell an asset at an agreed future time for an agreed price is called

A. spot contract. **B.** forward contract.

C. future contract. **D.** swap.

Q.31 When a forward contract is traded on an exchange, it is called

A. spot contract. **B.** future contract.

C. call option. **D.** put option.

Q.32 On 1 January you enter a contract to buy 1 million barrels of oil for $80 per barrel to be delivered on 1 March. The price of 1 March is $82 per barrel. Your gain is

A. $200. **B.** $20000.

C. $200000. **D.** $2000000.

Q.33 Allocating stock in popular new issues to manager of their important corporate clients is called

A. subscription. **B.** under-performance.

C. rights. **D.** spinning.

Q.34 Which of the following issues has the lowest total direct cost?

A. Straight bonds

B. Corporate stocks

C. All issues have same cost

D. None of these

Q.35 An increase in the value of a fixed asset is referred to as

A. depreciation.

B. appreciation.

C. market capitalization.

D. reverse depreciation.

Q.36 On an equity share of ₹ 10 the company has called up ₹ 8 but ₹ 6 have been received by the company is forfeited, the capital account should be debited by:

A. ₹ 10 **B.** ₹ 8 **C.** ₹ 6 **D.** ₹ 5

Q.37 Recovery of bad debt

A. increases net income.

B. decreases net income.

C. increases gross profit.

D. increases gross profit and net income.

Q.38 What does 'aged debtors analysis' signify?

A. Shows how long debts have been outstanding.

B. How old the customers are.

C. How long does a business take to repay the bank loans

D. Minimum number of old debtors.

Q.39 The return that is forgone by investing in the project rather than investing in financial markets at the same level of risk is called

A. internal rate of return.
B. capital saving.
C. opportunity cost.
D. opportunity saving.

Q.40 Redeemed debentures by issuing ordinary shares - Rate of return on ordinary shareholders' equity

A. increase.
B. decrease.
C. remain unchanged.
D. None of the above

Q.41 Purchased inventory on credit - Quick ratio.

A. Increase
B. Decrease
C. Remain unchanged
D. None of the above

Q.42 Issued additional ordinary shares for cash - Debt ratio

A. increase.
B. decrease.
C. remain unchanged.
D. None of the above

Q.43 Declared a cash dividend on ordinary shares - Dividend payout is

A. increase.
B. decrease.
C. remain unchanged.
D. None of the above

Q.44 Paid the cash dividend - Dividend yield is

A. increase.
B. decrease.
C. remain unchanged.
D. None of the above

Q.45 In the sales book for the month of January total of page 2 was carried forward to page 3 as Rs. 1,000 instead of Rs. 1200 and total of page 6 was carried forward to page 7 as Rs. 5600 instead of Rs. 5,000.

A. Debit Rs. 400 from the sales account and Credit Rs. 400 to suspense account.
B. Debit Rs. 400 from the suspense account and Credit Rs. 400 to sales account.
C. Debit Rs. 800 from the sales account and Credit Rs. 800 to suspense account.
D. Debit Rs. 800 from the suspense account and Credit Rs. 800 to sales account.

Q.46 Wages paid for the installation of machinery Rs. 500 was posted to wages account as Rs. 50

A. debit the machinery account with Rs. 450.
B. debit the machinery account with Rs. 500, Credit the wages account with Rs. 50, Credit the suspense account with Rs. 450.
C. credit the suspense account with Rs. 450.
D. credit the wages account with Rs. 50, Credit the suspense account with Rs. 450.

Q.47 Machinery purchased from R & Co. for Rs. 10,000 on credit was entered in Purchase Book as Rs. 6,000 and posted therefrom to R & Co. as Rs. 1,000.

A. Debit the machinery account with Rs. 6,000, Credit the purchases account with Rs. 6,000.
B. Debit the machinery account with Rs. 6,000, Debit the suspense account with Rs. 5,000, Credit the purchases account with Rs. 6,000.
C. Debit the machinery account with Rs. 10,000, Debit the suspense account with Rs. 5,000, Credit the purchases account with Rs. 6,000.
D. Debit the machinery account with Rs. 10,000, Debit the suspense account with Rs. 5,000, Credit the purchases account with Rs. 6,000, Credit the R & Co. account with Rs. 9,000.

Q.48 One way to obtain earnings forecasts is the mechanical procedure known as__________.

A. Cross-reference analysis
B. Exponential trending
C. Time series analysis
D. Data mining

Q.49 Goods returned to Ram Rs. 1,000 were recorded in Sales Book.

A. Debit the sales account with Rs. 1,000.
B. Credit the purchases return account with Rs. 1,000.
C. Debit the sales account with Rs. 1,000, Credit the purchases return account with Rs. 1,000.
D. Credit the purchases return account with Rs. 2,000.

Q.50 The date of settlement for a foreign exchange transaction is referred to as

A. clearing date.
B. swap date.
C. maturity date.
D. value date.

Q.51 Who are the real owners of a company?

A. Government
B. Board of Directors
C. Equity shareholders
D. Debentureholders

Q.52 The liability of members of a Company is

A. Limited
B. Unlimited
C. Stable
D. Fluctuating

Q.53 What are the limits of number of members in a Private Company?

A. Fifty
B. Seven
C. Twenty
D. Two hundred

Q.54 Shareholders receive from the company

A. interest.
B. commission.
C. profit.
D. dividend.

Q.55 The estimated value of an asset at which it can be dispose of after a given no. of years of useful life is called

A. depreciated value.
B. written down value.
C. salvage or residual value.
D. net value.

Q.56 The relationship between two financial variables can be expressed in

A. pure ratio.
B. percentage.
C. rate or time.
D. either of the above.

Q.57 Which A/c is opened when Trial Balance doesn't tally?

A. Trading A/c
B. Purchase A/c

C. Suspense A/c   **D.** Capital A/c

Q.58 In what time will the simple interest on Rs. 1000 at 3% per annum be the same as that on Rs. 1500 at 6% per annum in 3 years?

A. 6 years   **B.** 8 years   **C.** 9 years   **D.** 5 years

Q.59 A Man lends Rs. 1540 for five years and Rs. 1800 for four years. If he gets Rs. 1788 as interest on both amounts. what is the rate of interest?

A. 10 percent   **B.** 12 percent
C. 15 percent   **D.** 8 percent

Q.60 Find the compound interest on Rs. 10000 at 12% rate of interest for 1 year, compounded half- yearly.

A. 1236   **B.** 1326   **C.** 1623   **D.** 1632

Q.61 With compound interest, a sum of money amounts to Rs. 1,452 in 2 years and Rs. 1,597.20 in 3 years. What is the rate of interest per annum?

A. 9%   **B.** 12%
C. 10%   **D.** None of these

Q.62 A bank reconciliation statement is prepared by _________.
A. Creditors
B. Bank
C. Account holder in a bank
D. Debtors

Q.63 A company having a share capital can _________ its subscribed capital by issue of further shares to persons who are holders of equity shares of the company in proportion to the paid up share capital on those shares, by sending a letter of offer.
A. Increase   **B.** Decrease
C. Remain unchange   **D.** None of the above

Q.64 Cash received from debtors is _________________.
A. Sources of funds
B. Sources of cash
C. Application of funds
D. No flow of fund

Q.65 Sale of goods on a cash basis
A. increase.   **B.** decrease.
C. remain unchange   **D.** None of the above

Q.66 In debenture, interest payable is
A. transferred to general reserve.
B. transferred to falling fund investment account.
C. charged against the firm's profits.
D. appropriation of the company's profits.

Q.67 Reconciliation of overcasting on receipts side of cash book
A. increases the balance in the cash book.
B. increases the balance in the passbook.
C. decreases the balance in the cash book.
D. decreases the balance in the passbook.

Q.68 The one item listed below that would warrant the least amount of consideration in credit and collection policy decisions is the
A. quality of accounts accepted.
B. quantity discount is given.
C. a cash discount is given.
D. level of collection expenditures.

Q.69 What services are offered by correspondent banks? (i) International wire transfers, (ii) Cheque clearing, (iii) Cash/fund transfers
A. Only (i) and (ii)   **B.** Only (i) and (iii)
C. Only (ii) and (iii)   **D.** (i), (ii) and (iii)

Q.70 The possibility of loss on account of a default by a borrower in repayment of his obligation on time, is called
A. credit risk.   **B.** market risk.
C. default risk.   **D.** operational risk.

Q.71 An investor invested Rs.7.50 lakh in a project that gives a profit of Rs.2 lakh in the 1st year, Rs.2.60 lakh in the 2nd year, and Rs.4.50 lakh in the 3rd year. At a 10% discount rate, what is the present value of the cash inflows?
A. Rs.7.15 lakh.   **B.** Rs.7.25 lakh.
C. Rs.7.35 lakh.   **D.** Rs.7.45 lakh.

Q.72 Wages paid to the laborer for construction of factory building is a capital expenditure because (i) it increases the earning capacity, (ii) the benefit is for a long period, (iii) it is non-recurring.
A. Only (i) and (ii)   **B.** Only (i) and (iii)
C. Only (ii) and (iii)   **D.** (i), (ii) and (iii)

Q.73 The rate of return earned by an investor who purchases the bond and holds it till it matures is called
A. rate of return.
B. the current yield of the bond.
C. yield to maturity.
D. Any of the above

Q.74 The double-entry accounting system -
(a) Keeps a complete record of business transactions.
(b) It ensures arithmetical accuracy.
(c) The balance sheet can be prepared at the end of the year only by using this system.
(d) Easy to detect frauds and errors in this double-entry system.
A. a to d all   **B.** Only a, b and c
C. Only b, c and d   **D.** a, b, and c only

Q.75 When the balance as per the cash book is the starting point, in the reconciliation, the number of cheques issued and not presented are
A. subtracted.
B. added.
C. either added or subtracted.
D. None of the above

Q.76 Companies profit divided among shareholders is
A. interest.   **B.** reserve.

C. dividend.   **D.** surplus.

Q.77 According to the accounting equation assets are equal to
A. liabilities.
B. liabilities and equities.
C. equities.
D. None of these

Q.78 Which of the following expenses and their type does not match?
A. Cost of replacement of defective part of a machinery – Revenue Expense.
B. The professional fee paid in connection with the acquisition of leasehold premises- capital expenditure.
C. Purchase of land and building– capital expenses.
D. Traveling expenses incurred by the Chief Executive of a company in connection with the purchase of costly equipment – capital expenses.

Q.79 What does the accounting cycle represent a series of steps that a business uses?
A. To record and classify the transactions.
B. Make entries into the journal.
C. To record and classify the transactions.
D. All of these.

Q.80 Which of the following errors will affect the Trial Balance?
A. The total of the Sales Book has not been posted to the Sales Account.
B. paid as installation charges of a new machine has been debited to Repairs Account.
C. Goods costing taken by the proprietor for personal use have been debited to Debtors' Account.
D. paid for repairs to building have been debited to Building Account.

Q.81 At the time of forfeiture of shares the share capital account is debited with
A. face value.   **B.** called up value.
C. paid up value.   **D.** issued value.

Q.82 When the required rate of return is equal to the coupon rate, the value of the bond is
A. less than face value.
B. more than face value.
C. equal to face value.
D. maturity value.

Q.83 Which of the following Bank Employee styles arousing suspicion? (i) Lavish Lifestyle cannot be supported by his/her salary, (ii) Avoidance of long leave/vacation, (iii) Repeated negligence in observance of rules.
A. Only (i) and (ii)   **B.** Only (i) and (iii)
C. Only (ii) and (iii)   **D.** (i) (ii) and (iii)

Q.84 What is the Penalty to be imposed on banks for deficiencies in exchange of notes and coins/remittances sent to RBI/operations of currency chests etc. with respect to shortages in soiled note remittances and currency chest balances for notes in denomination up to Rs.50?
A. Rs. 50 per piece in addition to the loss.

B. Rs. 25 per piece in addition to the loss.
C. Rs. 20 per piece in addition to the loss.
D. Rs. 10 per piece in addition to the loss.

Q.85 The responsibility of ensuring the quality and genuineness of cash loaded at ...... would be that of the Sponsor Bank. (i) White Label ATM's, (ii) Brown Label ATM's.
A. Only (i)   **B.** Only (ii)
C. Either (i) or (ii)   **D.** Both (i) and (ii)

Q.86 Which of the following formula for calculation of compounded interest is not matched?
A. $P(1+r)=$ for calculation of annual compounding.
B. $P(1+(r/4))=$ for calculation of quarterly compounding.
C. $P(1+(r/2))=$ for calculation of half-yearly compounding.
D. $P(1+(r/4))=$ for calculation of weekly compounding.

Q.87 In view to controlling them and assessing the profitability and efficiency of the enterprise. (i) costing principles, (ii) costing methods, (iii) costing techniques.
A. Only (i) and (ii)   **B.** Only (i) and (iii)
C. Only (ii) and (iii)   **D.** (i), (ii) and (iii)

Q.88 Debenture carrying charge on the particular asset on the company is known as
A. fixed.   **B.** mortgage.
C. naked.   **D.** floating.

Q.89 Operating profit is
A. profit after deducting financial costs.
B. profit after deducting taxes.
C. profit after deducting normal operating expenses including depreciation.
D. equal to net profit.

Q.90 A change in accounting policy is justified when it is to:
A. Comply with the accounting standards
B. Ensure more appropriate presentation of the financial statements
C. Comply with legal or statutory requirements
D. All of these

Q.91 The accounting principle that states companies and owners should be accounted for separately is:
A. Business entity concept
B. Going concern concept
C. Monetary unit concept
D. Periodicity assumption

Q.92 To ensure that a company is following the Accounting Standards in India, is the duty of which of the following?
A. Company management.
B. Company Secretary.
C. Auditors of the company.
D. All the above

Q.93 The accounting entry required when the bank advises that a bank loan has been approved
A. debit Cash Account credit Bank Loan Account.
B. debit Bank Account credit Bank Loan Account.

C. debit Cash Account credit Bank Account.
D. debit Bank Account credit Cash Account.

Q.94 Cash Flow Statement is also known as
A. statement of Changes in Financial Position on a Cash basis.
B. statement accounting for variation in cash.
C. Both A and B
D. None of the above

Q.95 Profit for the objective of calculating a ratio may be taken as
A. profit before tax but after the interest.
B. profit before interest and tax.
C. profit after interest and tax.
D. All of the above

Q.96 The working capital financing policy that subjects the firm to the greatest risk of being unable to meet the firm's maturing obligations is the policy that finances
A. fluctuating current assets with long-term debt.
B. permanent current assets with long-term debt.
C. permanent current assets with short-term debt.
D. fluctuating current assets with short-term debt.

Q.97 Determining the appropriate level of working capital for a firm requires
A. evaluating the risks associated with various levels of fixed assets and the types of debt used to finance these assets.
B. changing the capital structure and dividend policy for the firm.
C. maintaining short-term debt at the lowest possible level because it is ordinarily more expensive than long term debt.
D. offsetting the profitability of current assets and current liabilities against the probability of technical insolvency.

Q.98 Compared to other firms in the industry, a company that maintains a conservative working capital policy will tend to have a
A. a greater percentage of short-term financing.
B. greater risk of needing to sell current assets to repay debt.
C. greater risk of needing to sell current assets to repay debt.
D. higher total asset turnover.

Q.99 From the following which is a method for the preparation of Trial Balance.
A. Balance Method
B. Total Method
C. Total-cum-Balance Method
D. All of the above

Q.100 Which of the following is the most common cause of bad debt?
A. Debtor refusal to repayment.
B. Debtor left the country.
C. Debtor committed a crime.
D. Debtor declared to be bankrupt.

Q.101 Where banks open a bank account of a foreign student, pending the verification of local address, a/c shall be operated with a condition of allowing foreign remittances not exceeding or equivalent into the account and a cap of on aggregate in the same?
A. USD 500, Rs.25000
B. USD 10000, Rs.50000
C. USD 15000, Rs.75000
D. USD 20000, Rs.1 lakh

Q.102 In the balance sheet of a firm, the notes relating to those facts are included, that do not find a place in the accounting statements. This is due to
A. convention of materiality.
B. convention of conservatism.
C. convention of accounting of full disclosure.
D. convention of consistency.

Q.103 What type of accounts, do appear in the balance sheet?
A. Real and nominal
B. Real and personal
C. Personal and nominal
D. Real, personal, nominal

Q.104 Which liabilities are not included in the totals of a balance sheet but their mention is made in the balance sheet?
A. Intangible liabilities
B. Fictitious liabilities
C. Current liabilities
D. Contingent liabilities

Q.105 The historical cost in the context of inventory valuation includes. (a) cost of purchase (b) cost of conversion (c) other costs incurred for bringing the inventory.
A. a and b only   **B.** b and c only
C. a and c only   **D.** a to c all

Q.106 Returns of goods from the customers of the firm should be credited to _______ and debited to________
A. customer account, sales returns.
B. sales account, sales returns.
C. customer account, sales account.
D. sales returns, customer account.

Q.107 An entry on the left side of a nominal account represents
A. income or expenditure.
B. only income.
C. income or gain.
D. expense or loss.

Q.108 The _______ concept makes a distinction between the receipt of cash and right to receive it or payment of cash and obligation to pay cash.
A. realization system   **B.** cash concept
C. accrual concept   **D.** consistency concept

Q.109 Which of the following is a commonly used base to create the provision for doubtful debts?
A. Total purchases.
B. Total credit sales.

C. Total current assets.

D. Total current liabilities.

Q.110 Entry for the transaction which is recorded on both sides of the Cash Book is called

A. closing entry.　　　**B.** contra entry.

C. opening entry.　　　**D.** adjustment entry.

Q.111 If an account is classified as high risk, the fresh KYC documents are be obtained after _______ years.

A. 10 years　　**B.** 8 years　　**C.** 3 years　　**D.** 2 years

Q.112 As per KYC guidelines, which one of the following customers is having high risk?

A. Central Govt. employee

B. State Govt. employee

C. Small business man

D. Politically exposed person resident abroad.

Q.113 Petty expenses are recorded in which of the following Cash Book.

A. Petty Cash Book

B. Simple Cash Book

C. Two-Column Cash Book

D. Three-Column Cash Book

Q.114 Which of the following is not recorded in the partner's current accounts?

A. Drawings

B. Interest on Drawings

C. Partners salaries

D. Administrative expenses

Q.115 Timeframe for collection of outstation cheques in case of Cheques drawn on State Capitals.

A. 2 Days　　**B.** 7 Days　　**C.** 10 Days　　**D.** 14 Days

Q.116 Which one of the following is the method of goodwill valuation?

A. Average capital method

B. Super capital method

C. Capital intensity method

D. Super profit method

Q.117 Margin money required for Education Loan above Rs. 4 lakh up to Rs. 7.5 lakh for Studies abroad is:

A. 6 percent　　　**B.** 5 percent

C. 10 percent　　　**D.** 15 percent

Q.118 if the market price of the share at expiration is $100 and the exercise price is $80, then the value of a put option at expiration is

A. –$20.　　**B.** $0.　　**C.** $1.　　**D.** $20.

// Smart Answer Sheet //

Correct — Indicates percentage of students who answered questions correctly.

Skipped — Indicates percentage of students who skipped questions.

Q.	Ans.	Correct / Skipped	Q.	Ans.	Correct / Skipped	Q.	Ans.	Correct / Skipped	Q.	Ans.	Correct / Skipped	Q.	Ans.	Correct / Skipped
1	C	50.25 % / 15.75 %	17	C	21.25 % / 35.75 %	33	D	40.25 % / 24.75 %	49	D	31.5 % / 36.5 %	65	A	30.25 % / 34.75 %
2	B	54.25 % / 33.5 %	18	B	28.75 % / 34.5 %	34	D	13.5 % / 35.0 %	50	C	19.25 % / 34.25 %	66	D	9.75 % / 34.0 %
3	A	38.5 % / 30.5 %	19	A	53.0 % / 14.0 %	35	A	32.0 % / 32.0 %	51	C	48.5 % / 30.75 %	67	C	16.5 % / 35.25 %
4	A	17.5 % / 35.75 %	20	A	36.75 % / 29.25 %	36	B	42.0 % / 31.5 %	52	D	25.5 % / 29.75 %	68	C	18.5 % / 35.5 %
5	A	18.0 % / 35.25 %	21	B	46.5 % / 28.0 %	37	B	19.75 % / 35.5 %	53	C	47.75 % / 35.25 %	69	C	19.0 % / 35.5 %
6	B	28.0 % / 33.75 %	22	D	16.75 % / 34.5 %	38	A	17.25 % / 33.75 %	54	A	36.75 % / 33.75 %	70	B	11.5 % / 35.75 %
7	D	28.0 % / 35.25 %	23	A	39.0 % / 21.5 %	39	A	30.0 % / 35.25 %	55	D	34.25 % / 32.25 %	71	D	43.0 % / 24.25 %
8	D	24.25 % / 34.25 %	24	C	40.25 % / 35.5 %	40	C	18.25 % / 35.5 %	56	D	47.0 % / 35.0 %	72	A	46.25 % / 30.25 %
9	B	27.5 % / 35.25 %	25	A	32.25 % / 35.0 %	41	B	22.25 % / 28.25 %	57	C	32.5 % / 35.25 %	73	C	20.0 % / 37.0 %
10	B	28.25 % / 34.0 %	26	D	38.5 % / 34.5 %	42	B	20.5 % / 35.0 %	58	D	23.25 % / 34.0 %	74	D	37.5 % / 34.0 %
11	A	38.5 % / 31.5 %	27	B	29.5 % / 27.25 %	43	C	45.0 % / 30.75 %	59	C	54.25 % / 32.5 %	75	C	42.75 % / 34.75 %
12	D	18.75 % / 34.75 %	28	D	30.5 % / 35.75 %	44	B	18.5 % / 35.5 %	60	C	46.25 % / 30.5 %	76	A	49.75 % / 33.75 %
13	C	24.25 % / 29.0 %	29	C	42.75 % / 28.0 %	45	A	29.75 % / 28.75 %	61	B	33.25 % / 36.5 %	77	B	30.25 % / 35.5 %
14	D	50.5 % / 34.5 %	30	B	20.5 % / 34.75 %	46	C	14.0 % / 35.0 %	62	A	44.25 % / 34.5 %	78	C	51.75 % / 34.0 %
15	D	53.5 % / 30.0 %	31	B	29.5 % / 31.75 %	47	A	23.5 % / 32.5 %	63	C	27.75 % / 33.75 %	79	B	32.75 % / 25.25 %
16	D	52.75 % / 31.0 %	32	B	39.5 % / 30.75 %	48	B	39.25 % / 35.5 %	64	C	30.0 % / 35.25 %	80	D	32.0 % / 30.75 %

Q.	Ans.	Correct / Skipped		Q.	Ans.	Correct / Skipped		Q.	Ans.	Correct / Skipped		Q.	Ans.	Correct / Skipped		Q.	Ans.	Correct / Skipped
81	D	59.75 % / 28.75 %		89	D	43.75 % / 36.5 %		97	D	30.5 % / 35.5 %		105	B	13.0 % / 35.0 %		113	D	61.25 % / 27.25 %
82	A	26.0 % / 34.0 %		90	A	24.25 % / 35.0 %		98	C	13.0 % / 35.0 %		106	D	30.75 % / 35.0 %		114	D	53.5 % / 35.0 %
83	B	13.5 % / 35.0 %		91	C	40.75 % / 35.0 %		99	D	14.25 % / 34.25 %		107	D	46.0 % / 31.5 %		115	A	48.5 % / 33.5 %
84	C	36.0 % / 34.0 %		92	D	46.5 % / 35.0 %		100	C	13.75 % / 31.75 %		108	A	17.5 % / 35.0 %		116	D	27.5 % / 35.25 %
85	D	32.75 % / 35.5 %		93	A	25.5 % / 28.75 %		101	D	40.25 % / 35.25 %		109	D	39.25 % / 28.25 %		117	B	43.5 % / 26.75 %
86	A	23.25 % / 34.75 %		94	C	20.0 % / 35.5 %		102	D	31.0 % / 35.0 %		110	C	19.0 % / 34.25 %		118	D	18.75 % / 34.5 %
87	A	21.5 % / 35.25 %		95	B	35.25 % / 33.75 %		103	B	25.25 % / 35.75 %		111	B	27.5 % / 26.25 %		119	D	22.75 % / 26.25 %
88	D	50.5 % / 35.0 %		96	C	51.5 % / 34.0 %		104	C	33.75 % / 33.75 %		112	B	42.75 % / 35.5 %		120	B	10.25 % / 31.5 %

Performance Analysis

Avg. Score (%)	31.0%
Toppers Score (%)	99.0%
Your Score	

//Hints and Solutions//

1. A Bank Reconciliation Statement is the comparison of a bank statement (sent by the bank) with the Cashbook. In other words, the balance shown in the Pass Book given by the bank should tally with the balance of Bank Account Kept in his ledger or Cash Book (Bank Column).
Hence, the correct option is (C)

2. A cheque returned by a bank marked "NSF" means that there are not sufficient funds in your account. Non-sufficient funds (NSF) is a term used in the banking industry to indicate that a cheque cannot be honored because insufficient funds are available in the account on which the instrument was drawn.
Hence, the correct option is (B)

3. Bank Reconciliation Statement is prepared by the Accountant of business. A bank reconciliation statement is generally prepared by the company accountant or the bookkeeper with the purpose to compare the bank's records with your own company records. It is done on a monthly basis whenever a bank statement arrives.
Hence, the correct option is (A)

4. FIFO methods of inventory costing yield the highest taxable income. First-in, first-out, or FIFO, applies the earliest costs first. In rising markets, FIFO yields the lowest cost of goods sold and the highest taxable income.

Hence, the correct option is (A)

5. FIFO methods of inventory costing produce ending stock costs close to the market value of the inventory. FIFO (First-in, first-out) method is based on the perception that the first inventories purchased are the first ones to be sold. It is a cost flow assumption for most companies. Since the theory perfectly matches the actual flow of goods, therefore it is considered the right way to value inventory.

Hence, the correct option is (A)

6. LIFO inventory costing methods is supposed to issue the most recently purchased goods. LIFO, which stands for last-in-first-out, is an inventory valuation method that assumes that the last items placed in inventory are the first sold during an accounting year.

Hence, the correct option is (B)

7. Opening inventory + Net purchases = Cost of goods available for sale. The cost of goods available for sale equals the beginning value of inventory plus the cost of goods purchased.
Hence, the correct option is (D)

8. Cost of goods available for sale - closing inventory = Cost of goods sold.

Ending inventory is the value of goods available for sale at the end of an accounting period. It is the beginning inventory plus net purchases minus cost of goods sold.

Hence, the correct option is (D)

9. NRV or net realizable value of inventory is the expected selling price or market value fewer Expenses necessary to complete the sale. Net realizable value is generally equal to the selling price of the inventory goods less the selling costs (completion and disposal).
Hence, the correct option is (B)

10. Under the Standard cost method of inventory costing, a pre-determined cost is assigned to all items of inventory. A standard cost is described as a predetermined cost, an estimated future cost, an expected cost, a budgeted unit cost, a forecast cost, or as the "should be" cost. Standard costs are often an integral part of a manufacturer's annual profit plan and operating budgets.
Hence, the correct option is (B)

11. Term 'Credit' is broad with many different meanings in the financial world. It is generally defined as a contractual agreement in which a borrower receives something of value now and agrees to repay the lender at a later date-generally with interest.

Hence, the correct option is (A)

12. One of the first steps in analyzing a business transaction is deciding if the accounts involved increase or decrease. However, we do not use the concept of an increase or decrease in accounting. We use the words "debit" and "credit" instead of increase or decrease. The meaning of debit and credit will change depending on the account type. Debit simply means the left side; credit means the right side.

Hence, the correct option is (D)

13. The increase in assets and expenses are recorded on the debit side of an account. The increases in liabilities, equity, and revenues are recorded on the credit side of an account. Assets and expenses have normal balances on the debit side. Liabilities, equity, and revenues have normal balances on the credit side.

Hence, the correct option is (C)

14. General expenses, Financial expenses, and Selling expenses are paid out of Gross Profit.

Gross profit is the profit a company makes after deducting the costs associated with making and selling its products, or the costs associated with providing its services. Gross profit will appear on a company's income statement and can be calculated by subtracting the cost of goods sold (COGS) from revenue (sales).
Hence, the correct option is (D)

15. The land is NOT an example of intangible assets. An intangible asset is an asset that is not physical in nature.

Examples of intangible assets include goodwill, brand recognition, copyrights, patents, trademarks, trade names, and customer lists. You can divide intangible assets into two categories: intellectual property and goodwill.
Hence, the correct option is (D)

16. Loss is subtracted from the capital account and profit is added to the capital account.

According to a separate Accounting Entity concept, the business is considered separate from its owners. Hence any earnings made by the business are added to capital and any loss incurred is subtracted from the capital.

Hence, the correct option is (C)

17. Mr. Z's account will be credited if the business bought goods on credit from Mr. Z.

A cash account will be credited if a company purchases a building for cash. Cash is credited because cash is an asset account that decreased because cash was used to pay the bill.
Hence, the correct option is (B)

18. Interest on the loan paid by the business is an example of Revenue expense. Revenue expenditure is a cost that is charged to expense as soon as the cost is incurred

Revenue expenses are incurred when a company purchases products or services necessary for generating revenue in the short term. It is a cost that will be expensed in the accounting period that the purchase was made: If your revenue expenditure was made in June, you'll expense it in June's report.

Hence, the correct option is (A)

19. Office equipment account will be credited when a typewriter is sold that has been used in the office.

A long-term asset account reported on the balance sheet under the heading of property, plant, and equipment. Included in this account would be copiers, computers, printers, fax machines.

Hence, the correct option is (A)

20. The allocation of the cost of a tangible plant asset to expense in the periods, in which services are received from the asset, is termed as Depreciation. Depreciation is any method of allocating such net cost to those periods in which the organization is expected to benefit from the use of the asset. The asset is referred to as a depreciable asset.
Hence, the correct option is (B)

21. Credit sales will be shown on the debit side of the debtor's account. Credit sales mean allowances of goods to customers in order to pay in advance.

The debit is an entry on the left side of an account. Under the double-entry bookkeeping system, debits increase assets and expense and decrease liabilities, equity, and income (revenues).

Hence, the correct option is (D)

22. When one or both aspects of a transaction are recorded in the wrong class or category of account, it is called an Error of principle. An error of principle is an accounting mistake in which an entry is recorded in the incorrect account, violating the fundamental principles of accounting.

Errors of principle are often simply accounting entries recorded in the incorrect account. The amounts are often correct, unlike an error of original entry. Oftentimes, the error of principle is a procedural error, meaning that the value recorded is correct but the entries are made in the wrong accounts.
Hence, the correct option is (A)

23. Salaries of selling staff would not be considered as a component of 'cost' of stock. When investors purchase shares of stock, the price paid includes two components the price of the stock and the fee charged by the brokerage firm, called commission.
Hence, the correct option is (C)

24. A current asset is TRUE about the treatment of insurance premiums paid in advance. Current assets represent all the assets of a company that are expected to be conveniently sold, consumed, utilized, or exhausted through the standard business operations, which can lead to their conversion to a cash value over the next one year period.
Hence, the correct option is (A)

25. Both listed and non listed companies are types of Public Limited Companies.

A public company, publicly traded company, publicly held company, publicly listed company, or public limited company is a company whose ownership is organized via shares of stock which are intended to be freely traded on a stock exchange or in over-the-counter markets.

A non-listed company is defined in the AIFM Directive as "a company which has its registered office in the Union and the shares of which are not admitted to trading on a regulated market within the meaning of point (14) of Article 4(1) of" the MiFID Directive .
Hence, the correct option is (D)

26. The charter of a company that defines the limitations and powers of the company is called Articles of association. Articles of association are a document that specifies the regulations for a company's operations and defines the company's purpose. The document lays out how tasks are to be accomplished within the organization, including the process for appointing directors and the handling of financial records.
Hence, the correct option is (B)

27. Merchandise on hand at either the beginning or end of the accounting period is called Inventory.

Inventory is the array of finished goods or goods used in the production held by a company. Inventory is classified as a current asset on a company's balance sheet, and it serves as a buffer between manufacturing and order fulfilment.
Hence, the correct option is (D)

28. In the calculation of depreciation, all of the following items are actually estimates except Historical cost. A historical cost is a measure of value used in accounting in which the price of an asset on the balance sheet is based on its nominal or original cost when acquired by the company.

Hence, the correct option is (C)

29. American-style option contracts can be exercised at any time up to the option's expiration. Under certain circumstances, early exercise may be advantageous to the option holder. The type of option that can be exercised only at the date of expiration is classified as a European option. A European option is a version of an options contract that limits execution to its expiration date.
Hence, the correct option is (B)

30. A forward contract is an agreement between a buyer and seller of the contract that some asset—such as a commodity, currency, or stock—will be bought or sold for a specific price, on a specific day in the future (the expiration date).
Hence, the correct option is (B)

31. Forward contracts are agreements between two parties to exchange two designated currencies at a specific time in the future. These contracts always take place on a date after the date

that the spot contract settles and are used to protect the buyer from fluctuations in currency prices. When the forward contract is traded on an exchange, it is called a futures contract.
Hence, the correct option is (B)

32. On 1 January the price of oil is $80 per barrel
On 1 March the price of oil is $82 per barrel
Profit is $2 per barrel
The contract is for 1 million barrels. So, the total gain is $2
$\times$ 1000000
=$2000000
Hence, the correct option is (D)

33. The term spinning refers to the act of offering preferred customers shares in an initial public offering (IPO) by a brokerage firm or underwriter in order to keep or obtain their business. Spinning theoretically benefits the underwriter or brokerage firm, as well as the preferred customer to whom the shares are offered. The practice of spinning, also called IPO spinning, is both illegal and unethical. The act of spinning has nothing to do with spinning off—when a company breaks off one of its segments or divisions into a separate entity.
Hence, the correct option is (D)

34. A straight bond is the most basic of debt investments. It is also known as a plain vanilla bond because it has no additional features that other types of bonds might have. All other bond types are variations of or additions to standard straight bond features. For example, some bonds can be converted into shares of common stock, and others can be called or redeemed before their maturity dates. Special bonds such as convertible, callable, and puttable bonds are structured as straight bonds plus a call option or warrant.

As with all bonds, there is default risk, which is the risk that the company could go bankrupt and no longer honor its debt obligations, as well as interest rate risk as rate changes affect bond prices in the secondary market.

The standard features of a straight bond include constant coupon payments, face value or par value, purchase value, and a fixed maturity date. A straight bondholder expects to receive periodic interest payments, known as coupons, on the bond until the bond matures. At the maturity date, the principal investment is repaid to the investor. The return on principal depends on the price that the bond was purchased for. If the bond was purchased at par, the bondholder receives the par value at maturity. If the bond was purchased at a premium to par, the investor will receive a paramount less than his or her initial capital investment. Finally, a bond acquired at a discount to par means that the investor's repayment at maturity will be higher than his or her initial investment.
Hence, the correct option is (A)

35. An increase in the value of a fixed asset is referred to as appreciation. Appreciation, in general terms, is an increase in the value of an asset over time. The increase can occur for a number of reasons, including increased demand or weakening supply, or as a result of changes in inflation or interest rates.

Hence, the correct option is (B)

36. Shares are issued at a face value against which a certain amount is called up. The called up amount is credited to share capital account.

Once the shares are forfeited, a reversal entry need to be passed in books of account by debiting the share capital account by the amount of called up amount.
Hence, the correct option is (B)

37. Recovery of bad debt increases net income. Bad debt recovery is a payment received for a debt that was written off and considered uncollectible. The receivable may come in the form of a loan, credit line, or any other accounts receivable. Because it generally generates a loss when it is written off, bad debt recovery usually produces income.

Hence, the correct option is (A)

38. Aged debtors analysis shows how long debts have been outstanding. An aged debtors report is a totaled list of all the invoices your customers haven't yet paid you for, less any credit notes you've issued to your customers and not yet refunded them for.

Hence, the correct option is (A)

39. "Opportunity cost is the loss of potential gain from other alternatives when one alternative is chosen." In simple terms, the opportunity cost is the benefit not received as a result of not selecting the next best option. Opportunity cost is a key concept in economics, and has been described as expressing "the basic relationship between scarcity and choice".

The meaning of the concept of opportunity cost can be explained with the help of the following examples:

1. The opportunity cost of the funds tied up in one's own business is the interest (or profits corrected for differences in risk) that could be earned on those funds in other ventures.

2. The opportunity cost of the time one puts into his own business is the salary he could earn in other occupations (with a correction for the relative psychic income in the two occupations).

3. The opportunity cost of using a machine to produce one product is the earnings that would be possible from other products.

4. The opportunity cost of using a machine that is useless for any other purpose is nil since its use requires no sacrifice of other opportunities.

Hence, the correct option is (C)

40. Convertible debentures are converted into equity shares on maturity. The conversion date and rate of conversion are stated in the prospectus. The company does not redeem convertible debentures. Convertible debentures can be classified into fully convertible and partly convertible debentures. Redeemed debentures by issuing ordinary shares - Rate of return on ordinary shareholders' equity decrease.
Hence, the correct option is (B)

41. Quick Ratio Calculation The formula to calculate the quick ratio is:

$$QR = \frac{CE+MS+AR}{CL}$$

Or

$$QR = \frac{CA-I-PE}{CL}$$

where:

QR = Quick ratio

CE = Cash & equivalents

MS = Marketable securities

AR = Accounts receivable

CL = Current Liabilities

CA = Current Assets

I = Inventory

PE = Prepaid expenses

Here inventory and liability increases so Quick ratio decreases. Hence, the correct option is (B)

42. The debt ratio is also known as the debt to asset ratio or the total debt to total assets ratio. Hence, the formula for the debt ratio is total liabilities divided by total assets. The debt ratio indicates the percentage of the total asset amounts (as reported on the balance sheet) that is owed to creditors. Hence, the correct option is (B)

43. The journal entry to record the declaration of the cash dividends involves a decrease (debit) to Retained Earnings (a stockholders' equity account) and an increase (credit) to Cash Dividends Payable (a liability account). Hence, the correct option is (A)

44. Once you know how much a company has made in net income and paid out in dividends in a given time period, finding its dividend payout ratio is simple. Divide its dividend payments by its net income. The value you get is its dividend payout ratio. Hence, the correct option is (C)

45. Total carried forward from Page 2 to Page 3 is Rs. 200 less (Rs. 1,200 – Rs. 1,000 = Rs. 200).

Total carried forward from page 6 to page 7 is Rs. 600 more (Rs. 5,600 – Rs. 5,000 = Rs. 600). In total Rs. 400 (Rs. 600 – Rs. 200 = Rs. 400) credit balance is carried forward in surplus, the rectification entry would be to Debit Rs. 400 from the sales account and Credit Rs. 400 to the suspense account. Hence, the correct option is (A)

46. Wages paid for the installation of machinery was wrongly posted (debited) to wages account as Rs. 50, instead of crediting the machinery account with Rs. 500, the rectification entry would be to Credit the wages account with Rs. 50 to rectify the wrongly debited amount of Rs. 50 Debit the machinery account with Rs. 500.Credit the suspense account with the difference i.e. Rs. 500 – Rs. 50 = Rs. 450. Hence, the correct option is (B)

47. Machinery purchased from R & Co. on credit for Rs. 6,000 was wrongly recorded (debited) in the purchases book as Rs. 6,000 and posted (credited) to R & Co. as Rs. 1,000, the rectification entry would be to Credit the purchases account with Rs. 6,000 to rectify the wrongly debited amount of Rs. 6,000 Credit the R & Co. account with the remaining amount (Rs. 1,000 was already

credited) i.e. Rs. 10,000 – Rs. 1,000 = Rs. 9,000 Debit the machinery account with Rs. 10,000 Debit the suspense account with the difference. Rs. 6,000 + Rs. 9,000 – Rs. 10,000 = Rs. 5,000. Hence, the correct option is (D)

48. One way to obtain earnings forecasts is the mechanical procedure known as time series analysis. Time series analysis is a statistical technique that deals with time series data, or trend analysis. Time series data means that data is in a series of particular time periods or intervals.

Hence, the correct option is (C)

49. Goods returned to Ram were recorded (credited) in the Sales Book instead of crediting to the purchases return the book, the rectification entry would be to Debit the sales account with Rs. 1,000 to rectify the wrongly credited amount of Rs. 1,000 Credit the purchases return account with Rs. 1,000 to represent the transaction. Hence, the correct option is (C)

50. Value date, in finance, is the date when the value of an asset that fluctuates in price is determined. The value date is used when there is a possibility for discrepancies due to differences in the timing of asset valuation. Hence, the correct option is (D)

51. A shareholder, also referred to as a stockholder, is a person, company, or institution that owns at least one share of a company's stock, which is known as equity. Because shareholders are essentially owners in a company, they reap the benefits of a business' success. Hence, the correct option is (C)

52. The liability of the members of the company is limited to contribution to the assets of the company upto the nominal value of shares held by him. A member is liable to pay only the uncalled money due on shares held by him when called upon to pay and nothing more, even if liabilities of the company far exceeds its assets. On the other hand, partners of a partnership firm have unlimited liability i.e. if the assets of the firm are not adequate to pay the liabilities of the firm, the creditors can force the partners to make good the deficit from their personal assets. This cannot be done in case of a company once the members have paid all their dues towards the shares held by them in the company. Hence, the correct option is (A)

53. This type of entity limits the owner's liability to their ownership stake and restricts shareholders from publicly trading shares. Members: You can start a private limited company with a minimum of only 2 members (and a maximum of 200), as per the provisions of the Companies Act 2013. Minimum 2 and Maximum 20 can only be a part of partnership firm while for a private limited company, 2 to 50 members in case of Private Company and Minimum 7 members in case of Public Company can be a part and in LLP's there have to be minimum 2 partners and there is no limit of a maximum number of partners. Hence, the correct option is (D)

54. Common shareholders possess the right to share in the company's profitability and gains from its stock price appreciation. Shareholders may also share in a company's profits by receiving cash or stock payments from the company - called

dividends.
Hence, the correct option is (D)

55. Salvage value is sometimes referred to as disposal value, residual value, terminal value, or scrap value. The estimated salvage value is deducted from the cost of the assets in order to determine the total amount of depreciation expenses that will be reported during the asset's useful life. The price at which a fixed asset is expected to be sold at the end of its useful life is called disposal value.
Hence, the correct option is (C)

56. Ratios show the relationship between two numbers. The accounting ratio shows the relationship between two accounting figures. Ratio analysis is the process of computing and presenting the relationships between the items in the financial statements. It is an important tool of financial analysis because it helps to study the financial performance and position of a concern.
FORMS
There are three different forms in which an accounting ratio can be expressed
1. Pure ratio: A pure ratio is a simple division of one number by another. The relationship between current asset $\&$ current liabilities are expressed in this way.
2. Percentage: Certain accounting ratio becomes more meaning full if expressed as a percentage. The relationship between profit and sales is expressed in this way
3. Rate: Sometimes ratios are expressed as rates i.e. 'number of times" over a certain period. relationship between stock and sales is expressed in this way.

Hence, the correct option is (D)

57. Suspense accounts are used when your trial balance is out of balance or when you have an unidentified transaction. The suspense account is a general ledger account that acts as a holding account until the error is discovered or the unknown transaction is identified.
Hence, the correct option is (C)

58. given, Rs. 1000 at 3%

Rs. 1500 at 6% in 3 year

to find n=?

Let time is n years $\dfrac{(1000 \times 3 \times n)}{100} = \dfrac{(1500 \times 6 \times 3)}{100}$

$n = 9$ years

Hence, the correct option is (C)

59. given, Rs. 1540 for 5 year

Rs. 1800 for 4 year

Rs. 1788 as interest on both amounts.

to find interest rate

Let the interest rate be r%

We know that, S.I= $\dfrac{PTR}{100}$

$\Rightarrow \dfrac{(1540 \times 5 \times r)}{100} + \dfrac{(1800 \times 4 \times r)}{100} = 1788$

$\Rightarrow r = \dfrac{178800}{14900} = 12\%$
Hence, the correct option is (B)

60. $P = Rs.\,10000$
$T = 1$ year
$R = 12\%$ p.a.
Compounded half yearly $n = 2$
$\therefore A = P\left[1 + \dfrac{R}{n}\right]^{nT}$
$= 10000\left[1 + \dfrac{0.12}{2}\right]^{2 \times 1}$
$= 10000\left[\dfrac{2.12}{2}\right]^{2}$
$= 10000 \times 1.06 \times 1.06$
$A = 11236$
$C \cdot I = A - P$
$= Rs.\,(11236 - 10000)$
$= Rs.\ 1236$
Hence, the correct option is (A)

61. Suppose principal $= Rs.P$ and rate $= R\%$
Given $A = Rs.\,1450$ for $N = 2$
$A = Rs.\,1597.20$ for $N = 3$
$\therefore P\left(1 + \dfrac{R}{100}\right)^{2} = 1,452$
$P\left(1 + \dfrac{R}{100}\right)^{3} = 1,597.20$
Dividing (2) by (1), we get
$1 + \dfrac{R}{100} = \dfrac{1,597.20}{1,452}$
$\dfrac{R}{100} = \dfrac{1,597.20}{1.452} - 1 = \dfrac{145.20}{1,452} = 10\%$
Hence, the correct option is (C)

62. Whenever money is deposited in the bank or withdrawn from the bank it is recorded in two places.

The passbook maintained by the bank.

The cash book (bank column) maintained by the account holder.

These two books are opposites of each other which means if one shows a credit balance then the other would reflect a debit balance of the exact same amount. But due to reasons like timing differences, the balances of both these books do not match. Now, it is not practical and feasible for the bank to reconcile the account balances of each and every account holder so, the account holder prepares a bank reconciliation statement for his account maintained in the bank.

Hence, the correct option is (C).

63. A company (including Private company) having a share capital can increase its subscribed capital by issue of further shares to persons who are holders of equity shares of the company in proportion to the paid up share capital on those shares, by sending a letter of offer.

Further Issue of Share Capital-
Whereat any time, a company having a share capital proposes to increase its subscribed capital by the issue of further shares, such

shares shall be offered-
(a) To persons who, at the date of the offer, are holders of equity shares of the company in proportion, as nearly as circumstances admit, to the paid-up share capital on those shares by sending a letter of offer subject to the following conditions, namely:
(i) The offer shall be made by notice specifying the number of shares offered and limiting a time not being less than fifteen days and not exceeding thirty days from the date of the offer within which the offer, if not accepted, shall be deemed to have been declined;
(ii) Unless the articles of the company otherwise provide, the offer aforesaid shall be deemed to include a right exercisable by the person concerned to renounce the shares offered to him or any of them in favour of any other person, and the notice referred to in clause (i) shall contain a statement of this right;
(iii) After the expiry of the time specified in the notice aforesaid, or on receipt of earlier intimation from the person to whom such notice is given that he declines to accept the shares offered, the Board of Directors may dispose of them in such manner which is not dis-advantageous to the shareholders and the company;
(b) To employees under a scheme of employees' stock option, subject to [special resolution] passed by company and subject to such conditions.
Hence, the correct option is (A)

64. When cash payment is received from the debtor, cash is increased and the accounts receivable is decreased. When recording the transaction, cash is debited, and accounts receivable are credited. A debtor is a person, company, or other entity that owes money. In other words, the debtor has a debt or legal obligation to pay the amount owed. So the cash received from debtors is no flow of funds.

Hence, the correct option is (D).

65. The entry for goods sold on cash is Cash has been debited because sales cash has been received by the firm through sales. so our asset (cash) has increased. when an asset is increased it has to be debited. When you sell something to a customer who pays in cash, debits your Cash account and credits your Revenue account. This reflects the increase in cash and business revenue. Realistically, the transaction total won't all be revenue for your business. It will also involve sales tax, which is a liability.
Hence, the correct option is (C)

66. Interest on debenture is a charge opposite to the profit of the enterprise and has to be paid whether the enterprise has acquired any profit. According to the Income Tax Act, 1961, an enterprise must deduct income tax at the recommended rate from the interest payable on debentures if it surpasses the guided limit.

Hence, the correct option is (C)

67. Reconciliation of overcasting on receipts side of cash book decreases the balance in the cash book. It depends on which side of the cash-book is overcast by Rs. 100 In case the credit side of the cash book is overcast then that means the excess amount has been shown as paid and hence should be added back while calculating balance as per pass book in.

Hence, the correct option is (C)

68. Answer (B) is correct. A quantity discount is an attempt to increase sales by reducing the unit price on bulk purchases. It concerns only the price term of an agreement, not the credit term, and thus is unrelated to credit and collection policy.

Answer (A) is incorrect because The quality of accounts is important to credit policy since it is inversely related to both sales and bad debts.

Answer (C) is incorrect because Offering a cash discount improves cash flow and reduces receivables and the cost of extending credit.

Answer (D) is incorrect because The level of collection expenditures must be considered when implementing a collection policy. The marginal cost of a credit and collection policy should not exceed its revenue.
Hence, the correct option is (B)

69. Correspondent banks offer the following services, such as Treasury, clearance of cheques, drawing of demand drafts, process documentation, foreign exchange, financing, managing international investments, and more. The correspondent bank charges a specific fee for its services to the respondent bank.
Hence, the correct option is (D)

70. Credit risk is the risk of default on a debt that may arise from a borrower failing to make required payments. In the first resort, the risk is that of the lender and includes lost principal and interest, disruption to cash flows, and increased collection costs.

Credit risk is the possibility of a loss resulting from a borrower's failure to repay a loan or meet contractual obligations. Traditionally, it refers to the risk that a lender may not receive the owed principal and interest, which results in an interruption of cash flows and increased costs for collection.
Hence, the correct option is (A)

71. The discount rate is 10%.

So, for first year $1+0.1 = 1.1$.

For second year it is $1.1^2 = 1.21$

For 3rd year it is $1.1^3 = 1.331$.

$$\frac{2}{1.1} = 1.82, \frac{2.6}{1.21} = 2.15, \frac{4.5}{1.331} = 3.38.$$ Total is 7.35 lakhs.

Then find NPV by substracting cash outflow and inflow. We get a negative cash inflow. Hence there is a loss.
Hence, the correct option is (C)

72. (i) Expenses incurred for extension of railway tracks in the factory area should be treated as a Capital Expenditure because it will yield benefit for more than one accounting period.

(ii) Wages paid to machine operators should be treated as a Revenue Expenditure as it will yield benefit for the current period only.

(iii) Installation costs of new production machine should be treated as a Capital Expenditure because it will benefit the business for more than one accounting period.

(iv) Materials for an extension to foremen's offices in the factory should be treated as a Capital Expenditure because it will benefit the business for more than one accounting period.

(v) Rent paid for the factory should be treated as a Revenue Expenditure because it will benefit only the current period.

(vi) Payment for computer time to operate a new store's control system should be treated as Revenue Expenditure because it has been incurred to carry on the normal business.

(vii) Wages paid for building foremen's offices should be treated as a Capital Expenditure because it will benefit the business for more than one accounting period.
Hence, the correct option is (D)

73. Yield to maturity (YTM) is the overall interest rate earned by an investor who buys a bond at the market price and holds it until maturity. The concept of yield-to-maturity (YTM) is one of the widely used tools in bond investment management. Arithmetically, YTM is the single discount factor that makes the present value of future cash flows from bonds equal to the current price of the bond. Intuitively, YTM is the rate of return, which an investor can expect to earn if the bond is held till maturity.
Hence, the correct option is (C)

74. Double Entry System

This is the more traditional and conventional system for recording transactions in financial accounting. This is a scientific method that has some rules and principles which must be followed. The basic essence of the double-entry system is that every transaction will affect two accounts. This is known as the debit and credit rule – every credit entry, there must be a corresponding debit entry.

The double entry system is widely used and recognized in the accounting world. Some salient features of this system are,

- All three types of accounts are maintained in this system – real, nominal and personal

- The arithmetic accuracy of the financial records are verified by preparing the trial balance

- The system does not have many modifications.

- It allows for the preparation of the balance sheet which will reflect the financial position of the organization

- Easy to detect frauds and errors in this double-entry system.

Hence, the correct option is (A)

75. In case of cheques issued but not presented for payment, the entry for the same would be entered in the cash book as soon as the cheques are issued by the account holder as a result the cash book balance would be less than the passbook balance. So, while preparing a reconciliation statement if balance as per cash book is the starting point. cheques issued but not presented for payments are added.
Hence, the correct option is (B)

76. A dividend is a distribution of profits by a corporation to its shareholders. When a corporation earns a profit or surplus, it is able to pay a proportion of the profit as a dividend to

shareholders. Any amount not distributed is taken to be re-invested in the business (called retained earnings).
Hence, the correct option is (C)

77. From the accounting equation, we see that the number of assets must equal the combined amount of liabilities plus the owner's (or stockholders') equity. Owner's equity or stockholders' equity is the amount left over after liabilities are deducted from assets: Assets - Liabilities = Owner's (or Stockholders') Equity.
Hence, the correct option is (B)

78. Administrative expenses are expenses an organization incurs that are not directly tied to a specific function such as manufacturing, production, or sales. These expenses are related to the organization as a whole, as opposed to individual departments or business units. Administrative expenses include salaries of senior executives and costs associated with general services, for example, accounting and information technology. They tend to be unrelated to gross margins.
Hence, the correct option is (D)

79. The accounting cycle is a collective process of identifying, analyzing, and recording the accounting events of a company. The series of steps begin when a transaction occurs and end with its inclusion in the financial statements. The key steps in the eight-step accounting cycle include recording journal entries, posting to the general ledger, calculating trial balances, making adjusting entries, and creating financial statements.

Hence, the correct option is (D).

80. 'Total of Sales book has not been posted to Sales Account' will affect the Trial Balance because due to this Sales Account undercasts, which results in undercasting of credit side of Trial Balance.
Hence, the correct option is (A)

81. Forfeiture of shares is the cancellation of the shares of those shareholders who haven't paid the required value. When share forfeiture account is debited the called up value is considered because the company cancel only that amount which is demanded by them not that value which hasn't been demanded yet.
Hence, the correct option is (B)

82. When the market required rate of return equals the stated coupon rate, the price of the bond will equal its face value. Such a bond is said to be selling at par. If a bond sells at a discount, then P0 < par and YTM > coupon rate.
Hence, the correct option is (C)

83. Suspect Bank Employees
An employee leads a lavish lifestyle that cannot be supported by his or her salary.
An employee is reluctant to take a vacation.
An employee is associated with mysterious disappearances or unexplained shortages of significant amounts of bank funds
Negligence claims must prove four things in court: duty, breach, causation, and damages/harm. Generally speaking, when someone acts in a careless way and causes an injury to another person, under the legal principle of "negligence" the careless person will be legally liable for any resulting harm.
Hence, the correct option is (D)

84. Scheme of Penalties for bank branches based on performance in rendering customer service to the members of the public

Penalty

- For notes in denomination up to ₹ 50
- 50 per piece in addition to the loss
- For notes in denomination of above
- Equal to the value of the denomination per piece in addition to the loss.
- Shortages of 100 pieces and above per remittance shall be debited immediately. Penalty may be levied on reaching a limit of 100 pieces in a cumulative manner. Penalty on account of detection of counterfeit notes by RBI from soiled note remittance of banks and in currency chest balances shall be levied in terms of the instructions issued by DCM (FNVD) No. G $1/16.01.05/2018 - 19$ dated July 02, 2018, ₹ 50 per piece irrespective of the denomination
- Mutilated notes of 100 pieces and above per remittance shall be debited immediately. Penalty may be levied on reaching a limit of 100 pieces in a cumulative manner. The penalty of ₹ 5000 for each irregularity.
- Penally will be enhanced to ₹ 10,000 in case of repetition.
- The penalty will be levied immediately.

Hence, the correct option is (A)

85. Cash Management at the WLAs is the responsibility of the Sponsor Bank, who may if required, make necessary arrangements with other banks for servicing cash requirements at various places. WLAO is permitted to have more than one Sponsor Bank. While the cash would be owned by the WLAO, the responsibility of ensuring the quality and genuineness of cash loaded at such WLAs would be that of the Sponsor bank. At no point in time, the WLAO or his agents have access to the cash at the WLAs.
Hence, the correct option is (A)

86. Use this simple interest calculator to find A, the Final Investment Value, using the simple interest formula: A = P(1 + rt) where P is the Principal amount of money to be invested at an Interest Rate R% per period for t Number of Time Periods. Where r is in decimal form r=R/100 r and t are in the same units of time.
Hence, the correct option is (D)

87. Cost accounting provides daily, weekly or monthly statements of units produced, accumulated cost with analysis. Cost accounting system provides immediate information regarding the stock of raw material, semi-finished and finished goods. This helps in the preparation of financial statements.
Hence, the correct option is (D)

88. Those debentures which are secured by either a fixed charge or a floating charge on the assets of the company are called secured or mortgage debentures.

A fixed debenture, also known as a fixed charge debenture, is a debt that's issued against specific assets. Companies sign over specific assets, such as real estate or equipment, to the creditor as collateral for the loan.

Hence, the correct option is (A)

89. The term "operating profit" refers to an accounting metric measuring the profits a company generates from its core business functions, where the deduction of interest and taxes is excluded from the calculation.

The term "operating profit" refers to an accounting metric measuring the profits a company generates from its core business functions, where the deduction of interest and taxes is excluded from the calculation.
Hence, the correct option is (C)

90. A change in accounting policy is required by a new IFRS or a change to an existing IFRS / IAS and the transitional provisions of those standards allow or require the prospective application of a new accounting policy. The retrospective application of a change in accounting policy is impracticable.

Hence, the correct option is (D).

91. The business entity concept states that the transactions associated with a business must be separately recorded from those of its owners or other businesses. Doing so requires the use of separate accounting records for the organization that completely exclude the assets and liabilities of any other entity or the owner.

Hence, the correct option is (A).

92. An auditor is a person or a firm appointed by a company to execute an audit. To act as an auditor, a person should be certified by the regulatory authority of accounting and auditing or possess certain specified qualifications.
Hence, the correct option is (C)

93. When the loan is approved, the amount of the loan is transferred to the bank account. Since the amount is received, the bank balance increases, and hence the assets increase. Also since the amount is received on account of the loan given by the bank, liability has to be created to show the loan payable. Therefore, the entry shall be:

Bank A/c   Dr. (Loan received increases in the bank balance, hence debited)

To Bank Loan A/c (Loan is to be repaid to the bank, hence credited as liability)
Hence, the correct option is (B)

94. In financial accounting, a cash flow statement, also known as a statement of cash flows, is a financial statement that shows how changes in balance sheet accounts and income affect cash and cash equivalents, and breaks the analysis down to operating, investing, and financing activities.
Hence, the correct option is (C)

95. Ratio analysis will help validate or disprove the financing, investment, and operating decisions of the firm. They summarize the financial statement into comparative figures, thus helping the management to compare and evaluate the financial position of the firm and the results of their decisions.
Hence, the correct option is (D)

96. Fluctuating current assets can often be financed with short-term debt because the periodic liquidation of the assets provides funds to pay off the debt. However, financing permanent current assets with short-term debt is a risky strategy because the assets may not be liquidated in time to pay off the debt at maturity.

Answer (A) is incorrect because It is not particularly risky to finance working capital needs from long-term debt sources.

Answer (B) is incorrect because It is not particularly risky to finance working capital needs from long-term debt sources.

Answer (D) is incorrect because Financing fluctuating current assets with short-term debt is not as risky as financing permanent current assets with short-term.
Hence, the correct option is (C)

97. Working capital finance concerns the determination of the optimal level, mix, and use of current assets and current liabilities. The objective is to minimize the cost of maintaining liquidity while guarding against the possibility of technical insolvency. Technical insolvency is defined as the inability to pay debts as they come due.
Hence, the correct option is (D)

98. Compared to other firms in the industry, a company that maintains a conservative working capital policy will tend to have a greater risk of needing to sell current assets to repay debt. A firm following an aggressive working capital strategy would a. Hold a substantial amount of fixed assets.
Hence, the correct option is (C)

99. A Trial Balance is a statement that shows the total debit and total credit balances of accounts.It thus verifies the arithmetical accuracy of the postings in the ledger accounts. We will now study the methods of Preparation of Trial Balance – totals method, balance method, and total-cum-balance method.
Hence, the correct option is (D)

100. Debtor declared to be bankrupt is the most common cause of bad debt. Bad debt is a monetary amount owed to a creditor that is unlikely to be paid and, or which the creditor is not willing to take action to collect for various reasons, often due to the debtor not having the money to pay, for example, due to a company going into liquidation or insolvency.

Hence, the correct option is (D)

101. Banks may open a Non-Resident Ordinary (NRO) bank account of a foreign student on the basis of a higher passport (with appropriate visa & immigration endorsement) which contains the proof of identity and address in the home country along with a photograph and a letter offering admission from the educational institution.

Within a period of 30 days of opening the account, the foreign student should submit to the branch where the account is opened, a valid address proof giving the local address, in the form of a rent agreement or a letter from the educational institution as proof of living in a facility provided by the educational institution. Banks should not insist on the landlord visiting the branch for verification of rent documents and alternative means of verification of local address may be adopted by banks.

During the 30 days period, the account should be operated with a condition of allowing foreign remittances not exceeding USD 1,000 into the account and a cap of monthly withdrawal to Rs. 50,0001 -, pending verification of address.
Hence, the correct option is (B)

102. In the balance sheet of a firm, the notes relating to those facts are included, that do not find a place in the accounting statements. This is due to the convention of accounting of full disclosure.

The balance sheet is a formal document that follows a standard accounting format showing the same categories of assets and liabilities regardless of the size or nature of the business. Accounting is considered the language of business because its concepts are time-tested and standardized. Even if you do not utilize the services of a certified public accountant, you or your bookkeeper can adopt certain generally accepted accounting principles (GAAP) to develop financial statements. The strength of GAAP is the reliability of company data from one accounting period to another and the ability to compare the financial statements of different companies.
Hence, the correct option is (C)

103. The Balance sheet is the statement that shows the assets, equity, and liabilities of the company. It is divided under Assets and equity & liabilities heads. It shows balances of Personal and real accounts.

Whereas Trial Balance is the list of all balances of General Ledger Account. It is divided under Debit and Credit columns and It shows balances of Personal, real, and nominal account.
Hence, the correct option is (B)

104. Contingent liabilities are liabilities that may be incurred by an entity depending on the outcome of an uncertain future event such as the outcome of a pending lawsuit. These liabilities are not recorded in a company's accounts and shown in the balance sheet when both probable and reasonably estimable as 'contingency' or 'worst case' financial outcome. A footnote to the balance sheet may describe the nature and extent of the contingent liabilities. The likelihood of loss is described as probable, reasonably possible, or remote. The ability to estimate a loss is described as known, reasonably estimable, or not reasonably estimable. It may or may not occur.
Hence, the correct option is (D)

105. Cost of Purchase = All expenses for purchasing material and make the material in sellable condition. cost of sale = cost of purchase + administration expenses + selling expenses.

Conversion costs is a term used in cost accounting that represents the combination of direct labor costs and manufacturing overhead costs. In other words, conversion costs are a manufacturer's product or production costs other than the cost of a product's direct materials.

A historical cost is a measure of value used in accounting in which the value of an asset on the balance sheet is recorded at its original cost when acquired by the company. The historical cost method is used for fixed assets in the United States under generally accepted accounting principles (GAAP).
Hence, the correct option is (D)

106. Returns of goods from the customers of the firm should be credited to the customer account and debited to sales returns.

Goods sold to the customer can be returned by the customer due to various reasons. This has to be recorded in books of account as sales return.

The accounting entry will be as under:

Sales return A/c Dr, (Real A/c- Debit what comes in)

To Customer A/c (Person a/c- Credit the giver).
Hence, the correct option is (A)

107. An entry in the left-hand column of an account to record a debt; debits increase asset and expense accounts and decrease liability, income, and equity accounts. So An entry on the left side of a nominal account represents expense or loss.

In double-entry bookkeeping, debits and credits are entries made in account ledgers to record changes in value resulting from business transactions. A debit entry in an account represents a transfer of value to that account, and All those account types increase with debits or left side entries. Conversely, a decrease to any.
Hence, the correct option is (D)

108. Both transactions will be recorded in the accounting period to which they relate. Therefore, the accrual concept makes a distinction between the accrual receipt of cash and the right to receive cash as regards revenue and actual payment of cash and obligation to pay cash as regards expenses.
Hence, the correct option is (C)

109. Total credit sales is a commonly used base to create the provision for doubtful debts. The provision for doubtful debts is the estimated amount of bad debt that will arise from accounts receivable that have been issued but not yet collected. It is identical to the allowance for doubtful accounts.

Hence, the correct option is (B)

110. An entry that is made on both sides of a cash book is called Contra entry. In the dual entry accounting system, a Contra Entry is an entry which is recorded to reverse or offset an entry on the other side of an account. If a debit entry is recorded in an account, it will be recorded on the credit side and vice-versa.
Hence, the correct option is (B)

111. If an account is classified as high risk, the fresh KYC documents are be obtained after 2 years.

Banks will now be required to update KYC data only once in two years for high risk entities, and just once in 10 years for low-risk clients. Banks will now be required to update KYC data only once in two years for high risk entities, and just once in 10 years for low-risk clients.
Hence, the correct option is (D)

112. Banks seek KYC updates at different intervals for different clients based on their risk-categorization. Customers which banks feel could be of higher risk than any of these categories such as Politically Exposed Persons can be categorized even higher.
Hence, the correct option is (D)

113. A simple petty cash book is identical to a cash book. Any cash that a petty cashier receives is recorded on the debit or receipts side and any cash that he pays is recorded on the creditor payments side. In this type of Cashbook, all the expenses are recorded in one single column.
Hence, the correct option is (A)

114. In the case of a partnership type of ownership in a business, the partner's current account is prepared when capital is fixed. Transactions such as drawings, salary, and interest on capital and drawings are recorded. The balance of this account fluctuates every year. The balance can be both credit or debit.
Hence, the correct option is (D)

115. Timeframe for collection of outstation cheques drawn on state capitals/major cities/ other locations should be 7/10/14 days respectively. This timeframe is the outer limit and credit shall be afforded if the process gets completed earlier.
Hence, the correct option is (B)

116. Under the super profit method, goodwill is calculated on the basis of super-profits. Super profit is calculated by subtracting normal profit from average profit. Hence, the formula of super profit is average profit - normal profit.
Hence, the correct option is (D)

117. Margin money required for Education Loan above Rs. 4 lakh up to Rs. 7.5 lakh for Studies abroad is 15 percent.

For studies overseas, the required margin money increases to 15%. The banks also ask for collateral for loans above Rs 7.5 lakh. For loans above Rs 4 lakh up to Rs 7.5 lakh, a third-party guarantee is required. A collateral is asked for a loan exceeding Rs 7.5 lakh.

Hence, the correct option is (D).

118. A put option is said to have intrinsic value when the underlying instrument has a spot price (S) below the option's strike price (K). Upon exercise, a put option is valued at K-S if it is "in-the-money", otherwise its value is zero. Prior to exercise, an option has time value apart from its intrinsic value.
Hence, the correct option is (B)

Q.1 The portion of total deposits of a commercial bank which it has to keep with RBI in the form of cash reserves in termed as

A. CRR.

B. SLR.

C. Bank Rate.

D. Repo Rate.

Q.2 Which of the following is true?

A. Bank Reconciliation Statement(BRS) is an account

B. BRS is prepared by the bank

C. BRS shows causes of disagreement between cash book E passbook

D. BRS shows the only excess of cash book over passbook

Q.3 State Bank of India is a

A. Public Sector Bank.

B. Private Sector Bank.

C. Joint Sector Bank.

D. Non-Nationalised bank.

Q.4 For foreign Bank, priority sector lending targets is __ of net banking credit.

A. 32%

B. 36%

C. 40%

D. 44%

Q.5 In term of PMLA, records of cash transaction of Rs 10 lacs and suspicious transaction are required to be maintained for a period of

A. 5 years.

B. 10 years.

C. 15 years.

D. 25 years.

Q.6 Suspense Account in the trial balance will be entered in the ________.

A. manufacturing account

B. trading account

C. profit and loss account

D. balance sheet

Q.7 Real-Time Gross Settlement (RTGS) is management by

A. State Bank of India.

B. Reserve Bank of India.

C. Indian Bank Association.

D. Government of India.

Q.8 When depreciation is recorded by Charging to provision for depreciation account, the asset appears

A. at original cost.

B. at original cost less depreciation.

C. at market value.

D. at realizable value.

Q.9 Factors responsible for creating conditions for emergence and growth of monopoly are

A. control over strategic raw materials.

B. patent rights.

C. government licensing.

D. All of the above

Q.10 In the case of an inferior good, the income effect,

A. partially offsets the substitution effect.

B. is equal to the substitution effect.

C. reinforces the substitution effect.

D. more than offsets the substitution effect.

Q.11 A market in which only two firms exist is________.

A. oligopsony

B. oligopoly

C. duopoly

D. duopsony

Q.12 Value maximization theory fails to address the problem of

A. self-serving management.

B. risk.

C. uncertainty.

D. sluggish growth.

Q.13 Selling costs have to be incurred in case of

A. perfect competition.

B. monopolistic competition.

C. imperfect competition.

D. All of the above

Q.14 Which type of competition leads to exploitation of consumer?

A. Oligopoly

B. Monopolistic competition

C. Monopoly

D. All of the above

Q.15 The equilibrium is unstable and indeterminate under

A. Edgeworth model.

B. Cournot Model.

C. Sweezy Model.

D. Pareto Model.

Q.16 What are the decisions taken by government of India pertaining to Industrial Sector in the new industrial policy of 1991?

A. VRS to shed the excess load of workers

B. Disinvestment of public sector share holding

C. Referring sick units to BIFR

D. All of the above

Q.17 A monopolistic trade practise is deemed to be prejudicial to public interest except when

A. Authorized by Central Government.

B. Authorized by State Government.

C. Authorized by Supreme Court.

D. None of the above

Q.18 Which among these is not a method of privatization?

A. Denationalisation

B. Franchising

C. Sale of Business

D. All of the above

Q.19 The pre-liberalisation era of Indian Economy was under the grip of

A. unemployment.

B. under-employment.

C. fiscal deficit.

D. unfavourable and alarming balance of payment.

Q.20 Which among these can be a condition for the success of privatization?

A. Alternative institutional arrangements

B. Barriers to enter the market

C. Measurability of performance

D. All of the above

Q.21 Privatization of ownership through the sale of equity share is called

A. denationalization.

B. disinvestment.

C. contracting.

D. None of these

Q.22 Which among these is monopolistic trade practice?

A. Unreasonably limiting competition

B. Manufacturing only one product

C. Limiting technical Development

D. Selling only one product

Q.23 The Industrial policy resolution was passed first in_____.

A. 1931　　**B.** 1947　　**C.** 1956　　**D.** 1999

Q.24 Which of the following is true with respect to planning function?

A. To make a blue print of ideas and work

B. To tell the work allocation to all

C. Monitoring whether the things allocated are done properly

D. None of the above

Q.25 Each subordinate should have only one superior whose command he has to obey. This is known as

A. division of work.

B. exception principle.

C. unity of command principle.

D. authority responsibility principle.

Q.26 Inline and staff organization, the staff performs the function of

A. management.

B. advising management.

C. assigning responsibility.

D. All of the above

Q.27 The planning function is mainly performed at

A. top management level.

B. middle management level.

C. lower management level.

D. None of the above

Q.28 Which one of the following may not necessarily be an advantage of coordination?

A. Effective supervision

B. Unity of direction

C. Creative force

D. Summarization of all management functions

Q.29 Leadership is a function of all the following factors except

A. work group.

B. product or service.

C. leader.

D. situation.

Q.30 Which of the following is not true in respect of planning?

A. Planning is an intellectual activity.

B. Planning function is not performed by the top management.

C. Planning is related to objectives.

D. Planning is forward-looking.

Q.31 Which one of the following orders indicates the correct logical order of managerial functions?

A. Organizing, Planning, Directing, Staffing, Coordination and Control

B. Planning, Organizing, Staffing, Directing, Control and Coordination

C. Planning, Directing, Organizing, Staffing, Control and Coordination

D. Organizing, Planning, Staffing, Directing, Control and Coordination

Q.32 The process of recording transactions in different journals is called_____.

A. posting

B. entry making

C. adjusting

D. journalizing

Q.33 Minimum value of correlation is_____.

A. -2　　**B.** -1.5　　**C.** -1　　**D.** 0

Q.34 Files held on a storage device are identified by a special block of data held as the first block on the file. This block is called___.

A. file label

B. file scratch

C. file maintenance

D. None of these

Q.35 MIS stands for

A. Management Information System.

B. Multiple Information System.

C. Maximum Information System.

D. None of the above

Q.36 Graph of variables having non-linear relation will be

A. curved.

B. hyperbola.

C. straight Line.

D. None of the above

Q.37 The Horizontal curve represents the value of the coefficient of correlation to be_____.

A. positive

B. negative

C. zero

D. All of the above

Q.38 In case there is no relation between two variables. What will be the value of co-relation?

A. -2　　**B.** +1　　**C.** +2　　**D.** 0

Q.39 The sale of business asset on credit is recorded in

A. sales journal.

B. general journal.

C. cash receipt in the cash book.

D. nominal accounts.

Q.40 Karl Pearson's coefficient of correlation method of measuring correlation is_______.

A. graphic
B. mathematical
C. positional
D. None of the above

Q.41 Read the following statements:
(i) "Working capital is the number of funds necessary to cover the cost of operating the enterprise."
(ii) "Circulating capital means current assets of a company that are changed in the ordinary course of business from one form to another."
A. (i) and (ii) both are correct.
B. (i) and (ii) both are false.
C. (i) is correct but (ii) is false.
D. (i) is false but (ii) is correct.

Q.42 The cost of debt capital is calculated on the basis of
A. net proceeds.
B. annual Interest.
C. capital.
D. arumal Depreciation.

Q.43 Match List-I with List-II and select the correct answer using the codes given below the lists:

List-I	List-II
a. Matching approach	I. Dividend policy
b. Structural ratios	II. Inventory Management
c. Ordering quality	III. Financing Working Capital
d. Bonus-Shares	IV. Capital Structure

A.
a	b	c	d
I	II	III	IV

B.
a	b	c	d
III	IV	I	II

C.
a	b	c	d
III	IV	II	I

D.
a	b	c	d
II	I	III	IV

Q.44 Which of the following is not included in the assumption on which Myron Gorden proposed a model on Stock valuation?
A. Retained earning the only source of financing
B. Finite Life of the firm
C. Taxes do not exist
D. Constant rate of return on firms investment

Q.45 Examine the following statements:
(i) Payback period method measure the true profitability of a project.
(ii) Capital Rationing and capital budgeting mean the same thing.
(iii) Internal Rate of Return and Time Adjusted Rate of Return are the same thing.
(iv) Rate of Return takes into account the time value of money.
A. (i), (ii) and (iii) are correct.
B. (ii) and (iii) are correct.
C. Only (iii) is correct.
D. All (i), (ii), (iii) and (iv) are false.

Q.46 Which is called as Dividend Ratio Method?
A. Dividend Yield Method
B. Debt Equity Method
C. Asset Method
D. Equity Method

Q.47 If the current ratio is $2:1$ and working capital is Rs. $60,000$, What is the value of the current assets?
A. Rs. 60,000
B. Rs. 1,00,000
C. Rs. 1,20,000
D. Rs. 1,80,000

Q.48 Arrange the following steps involved in capital budgeting in order of their occurrence:
(i) Project Selection
(ii) Project appraisal
(iii) Project generation
(iv) Follow up
(v) Project execution
A. (ii), (iii), (i), (v), (iv)
B. (iii), (ii), (i), (v), (iv)
C. (i), (iii), (ii), (v), (iv)
D. (i), (ii), (iii), (v), (iv)

Q.49 Feedback and counseling involves
A. discuss the steps the employee can take for improvement.
B. provide support.
C. give critical and supportive feedback.
D. All of the above

Q.50 Which of the following is not true with regard to fixed assets?
A. They are acquired for using them in the conduct of business operations
B. They are not meant for resale to earn profit
C. They can easily be converted into cash
D. Depreciation at specified rates is to be charged on most of the fixed assets

Q.51 The concept of Human relations was developed by________.
A. Robert owen
B. V.V. Giri
C. Elton Mayo
D. Edwin B. Filippo

Q.52 Human Resource Management is concerned with
A. worker.
B. industrial relation.
C. field Staff.
D. all employees.

Q.53 The portion of the acquisition cost of the asset, yet to be allocated is known as
A. written down value.
B. accumulated value.
C. realizable value.
D. Salvage value.

Q.54 Dividends are usually paid on
A. called-up-capital.
B. subscribed-capital.
C. paid-up-capital.
D. issued capital.

Q.55 Assertion {A} Labour always get a major share of productivity gains.
Reason {R} Partial stoppage of work by workers amounts to strike.
A. (A) is true but (R) is false
B. (R) is true but (A) is false
C. (A) and (R) both are true
D. (A) and (R) both are false

Q.56 Objectives of training is________.

A. increased morale
B. increased productivity
C. favourable reaction to change
D. All of the above

Q.57 Present value is equivalent to

A. interest.
B. principal amount.
C. amount.
D. All of the above

Q.58 Promotion mix is the particular combination of promotional tools used by a company to _____ with its audiences.

A. communicate
B. help
C. purchasing decision
D. plan

Q.59 Which is a base of green marketing?

A. Green house gas reduction market
B. Capital Flow
C. Programme
D. Product

Q.60 Instruments payable to order can be transferred or negotiated by

A. endorsement & delivery.
B. mere delivery.
C. encashment.
D. None of the above

Q.61 Which is not a form of Internet Marketing?

A. Online marketing
B. Internet advertising
C. E-mail writing
D. Product Mix and Branding

Q.62 When the consignee receives the goods from the consigner

A. goods are debited to goods received on consignment account.
B. no entry is to be passed.
C. credit consignor's personal account.
D. None of the above

Q.63 Which is the problem of marketing communication?

A. Distance
B. Hidden sources and data
C. Lack of trust
D. All of the above

Q.64 The marketing manager have to carry out their responsibilities integrating all these factors in the management_____.

A. process
B. objective
C. goals
D. opportunity

Q.65 Sales promotion includes all promotional activities other than advertising, personal selling and

A. publicity.
B. advertisement.
C. production.
D. coupon.

Q.66 Every business transaction affects at least ___ accounts.

A. one
B. two
C. three
D. infinite

Q.67 "Marketing is a human activity directed at satisfying needs and wants through exchange processes." Who said?

A. Philip Kotler
B. Hansi L. V.
C. Peter F. Drucker
D. D. S. Pauler

Q.68 Which is the factor of Pricing decisions?

A. Economic and Political Environment of the Country
B. Trade Traditions
C. Competition
D. All of the above

Q.69 Which is the part of the 'Product Planning' Image?

A. Total Quality Management
B. Risk
C. Credibility
D. All of the above

Q.70 Degree of financial leverage is a measure of relationship between _________.

A. EPS and EBIT
B. EBIT and quantity produced
C. EPS and quantity produced
D. EPS and sales

Q.71 The internet offers marketers a fast, versatile, and inexpensive?

A. Communication medium
B. Cost of production
C. Cost of construction
D. All of the above

Q.72 The concept of marketing mix involves to deliberate and careful choice of organisation product, price, promotion and place strategies and

A. policies.
B. planning.
C. concept.
D. All of these

Q.73 Pricing objectives is a combination of

A. product line promotion.
B. cash Recovery.
C. profit Maximisation.
D. All of the above

Q.74 Which of the following factors affects the planning of marketing programme?

A. Marketing Strategy
B. Marketing Mix
C. Demand Variable
D. All of the above

Q.75 Product line covers

A. departmental Stores.
B. one Price Retailer.
C. general Retailer.
D. All of the above

Q.76 The principal function of an electronic market is to facilitate the search for the______.

A. required product or service
B. required marketing

C. required market

D. All of the above

Q.77 Depreciation is decline in the value of _________.

A. tangible fixed assets

B. current assets

C. intangible fixed assets

D. debentures

Q.78 Discount allowed is a kind of deduction from

A. account payable.

B. account receivable.

C. cash account.

D. discount account.

Q.79 _____ is basically buying a security in one market and simultaneously selling it in another market at a higher price, thereby profiting from the temporary difference in prices.

A. Cross rates

B. Forward rates

C. Market Arbitrage

D. Foreign Exchange

Q.80 When the required rate of return is more than coupon rate, then bonds will sell at _____.

A. par value

B. discount

C. premium

D. None of these

Q.81 Which among the following is/are the factors that affect the computation of depreciation?

A. Cost and Residual Value

B. Estimated useful life

C. Method of depreciation

D. All of the above

Q.82 Discount allowed is______.

A. expense of business

B. income of business

C. loss of business

D. abnormal loss of business

Q.83 Which among the following is not a Fixed Assets?

A. Debtors

B. Plant and Machinery

C. Furniture

D. Land

Q.84 Which of the following accounts will be debited if the business's owner withdraws cash from the business for personal use?

A. Drawings

B. Cash

C. Business

D. Stock

Q.85 What does RTGS stands for?

A. Real Time Grant System

B. Real Time Gross Settlement

C. Real Time Grant Settlement

D. None of these

Q.86 _______ is an arrangement whereby the seller recovers an amount of sales bill from the financial intermediaries before it is due.

A. Bill discounting

B. Bailment

C. Banker's Lien

D. None of these

Q.87 Which concept assumes states that the transactions associated with a business must be separately recorded from those of its owners or other businesses?

A. Basic Accounting Concept

B. Going Concern Concept

C. Business Entity Concept

D. Dual Concept

Q.88 A scheme under which the company grants an option to an employee to apply for shares of the company at a pre-determined price?

A. Right Issue

B. Private Placement

C. Employee Stock Option Scheme

D. Bonus Shares

Q.89 Discount for quick repayment of debt is normally referred to as

A. trade discount.

B. prompt payment discount.

C. cash discount.

D. bulk discount.

Q.90 Operating Profit means ______.

A. profit before Interest

B. profit after Tax

C. profit before Deprecation

D. profit before Interest and Tax

Q.91 Sales on credit are recorded in which of the following journal?

A. Purchase journal

B. Sales journal

C. Purchase return journal

D. Sales return journal

Q.92 Trial Balance is ____.

A. an account

B. a statement

C. subsidiary book

D. principal book

Q.93 Sales and purchase journal doesn't record______.

A. credit sales

B. credit purchases

C. credit sales and purchases

D. cash sales and purchases

Q.94 Cash received from the debtor is recorded in which of the following specialized journals?

A. Purchase Journal

B. Sales Journal

C. Cash Receipts Journal

D. Cash Payments Journal

Q.95 Salary Account is _____.

A. real Account

B. nominal Account

C. personal Account

D. None of these

Q.96 Cash purchases are recorded in which of the following specialized journals?

A. Purchase Journal

B. Sales Journal
C. Purchase return journal
D. Cash payments journal

Q.97 A brief explanation recorded below every entry in General Journal is commonly known as_____.
A. narration
B. explanation
C. summary
D. other Information

Q.98 Purchase of plant and machinery is example of _______.
A. revenue expenditure
B. fixed asset expenditure
C. capital expenditure
D. None of these

Q.99 A credit note is a basis for recording a transaction in which of the following journals?
A. Purchase Journal
B. Sales Return Journal
C. General Journal
D. Cash Receipt Journal

Q.100 Transferring entries from journal to ledger account is commonly known as_____.
A. recording
B. transferring
C. posting
D. entry making

Q.101 If wages are paid for the construction of business premises _____ account is credited and _____ account is debited.
A. wages, cash
B. premises, cash
C. cash, wages
D. cash, premises

Q.102 Human resources will not appear in the balance sheet according to _____ concept.
A. accrual
B. going concern
C. money measurement
D. None of the above

Q.103 Provision for discount on debtors is calculated on the amount of debtors
A. before deducting provision for doubtful debts.
B. after deducting provision for doubtful debts.
C. before deducting actual debts. and provision for doubtful debts.
D. after adding actual bad and doubtful debts.

Q.104 Which of the following is not a Real Account?
A. Machinery Account
B. Goodwill Account
C. Equipment Account
D. Sales Account

Q.105 Value of goods withdrawn by the proprietor for his personal use should be credited to_____.
A. capital account
B. sales account
C. drawings account
D. purchases account

Q.106 Which of the following is incorrect?
A. Goodwill intangible asset
B. Sundry debtors-current asset
C. Loose tools tangible fixed asset
D. Outstanding expenses-current asset

Q.107 M/s Stationery Mart will debit the purchase of stationery to ______.
A. purchases account
B. general expenses account
C. stationery account
D. None of the above

Q.108 Small items like pencils, pens, files, etc. are written off within a year according to___________ concept.
A. materiality
B. consistency
C. conservatism
D. realization

Q.109 The business enterprise is separate from its owner according to _____.
A. money measurement concept
B. matching concept
C. entity concept
D. dual aspect concept

Q.110 The policy to anticipate no profit and provide for all possible losses arise due to the concept of _____.
A. consistency
B. disclosure
C. conservatism
D. matching

Q.111 According to which concept, the proprietor pays interest on drawings?
A. Accrual Concept
B. Conservatism Concept
C. Entity Concept
D. Dual Aspect Concept

Q.112 Cost concept basically recognises
A. fair market value.
B. historical cost.
C. realisable value.
D. replacement cost.

Q.113 If the Market value of closing inventory is less than its cost price, inventory will be is shown at ____.
A. marketable value
B. fair Market value
C. Both (A) and (B)
D. None of the above

Q.114 The Market price of good declined than the cost price. The concept thatplays a key role is ____.
A. materiality
B. going concern concept
C. realization
D. consistency

Q.115 Which one of the following concepts states that the publication or presentation of financial statements should not be delayed?
A. Objectivity concept
B. Timing concept
C. Timeliness concept
D. Reliability concept

Q.116 Which of the following provide frame work and accounting policies so that the financial statements of different enterprises become comparable?
A. Business Standards

B. Accounting Standards

C. Market Standards

D. None of the above

Q.117 Which of the following factor is not considered while selecting accounting policies?

A. Prudence

B. Substance over form

C. Accountancy

D. Materiality

Q.118 "Debit the receiver & credit the giver" is _____ account.

A. personal

B. real

C. nominal

D. All of the above

Q.119 Cash Account is a _____.

A. real account

B. nominal

C. personal

D. None of the above

Q.120 As per the accrual concept, which of the following is not true?

A. Revenue – Expenditure = Profit

B. Revenue – Profit = Expenditure

C. Sales + Gross Profit = Revenue

D. Revenue = Profit + Expenditure

// Smart Answer Sheet //

Correct   Indicates percentage of students who answered questions correctly.

Skipped   Indicates percentage of students who skipped questions.

Q.	Ans.	Correct / Skipped
1	A	68.75 % / 2.78 %
2	C	42.36 % / 19.45 %
3	A	69.79 % / 22.22 %
4	A	27.43 % / 21.88 %
5	B	48.26 % / 22.92 %
6	D	34.03 % / 22.91 %
7	B	65.97 % / 23.96 %
8	A	20.14 % / 23.96 %
9	D	60.07 % / 25.35 %
10	A	15.28 % / 27.08 %
11	C	57.29 % / 27.43 %
12	A	19.44 % / 27.78 %
13	B	14.24 % / 28.47 %
14	D	29.86 % / 28.47 %
15	A	27.08 % / 29.86 %
16	D	55.21 % / 28.82 %
17	A	36.11 % / 29.17 %
18	C	17.71 % / 29.86 %
19	D	30.9 % / 30.21 %
20	B	7.29 % / 28.47 %
21	B	45.83 % / 31.25 %
22	B	20.83 % / 30.91 %
23	C	37.15 % / 31.6 %
24	A	38.89 % / 30.9 %
25	C	34.72 % / 32.29 %
26	B	4.86 % / 32.64 %
27	A	53.82 % / 33.33 %
28	A	11.11 % / 33.33 %
29	B	36.46 % / 33.68 %
30	B	48.26 % / 33.34 %
31	B	35.76 % / 35.07 %
32	D	28.82 % / 35.76 %
33	C	30.21 % / 35.76 %
34	A	37.15 % / 35.07 %
35	A	48.96 % / 35.76 %
36	A	29.86 % / 35.76 %
37	C	18.06 % / 35.41 %
38	D	39.93 % / 35.42 %
39	A	38.19 % / 35.07 %
40	B	27.08 % / 35.77 %
41	B	5.9 % / 36.46 %
42	B	20.49 % / 36.45 %
43	C	41.67 % / 37.15 %
44	B	12.85 % / 38.19 %
45	A	23.96 % / 37.15 %
46	A	37.5 % / 36.46 %
47	C	40.97 % / 37.15 %
48	B	15.62 % / 37.5 %
49	D	50.0 % / 37.15 %
50	C	32.99 % / 37.15 %
51	C	25.35 % / 38.19 %
52	D	50.0 % / 37.5 %
53	A	18.06 % / 37.15 %
54	C	31.6 % / 37.84 %
55	B	21.53 % / 37.5 %
56	D	51.74 % / 36.45 %
57	B	22.92 % / 37.5 %
58	A	36.81 % / 37.5 %
59	D	17.36 % / 37.5 %
60	A	42.36 % / 37.5 %
61	D	44.1 % / 37.5 %
62	B	16.32 % / 38.19 %
63	D	48.26 % / 38.2 %
64	A	23.61 % / 38.2 %
65	A	24.31 % / 38.54 %
66	B	48.61 % / 38.54 %
67	A	28.12 % / 38.89 %
68	D	46.53 % / 38.19 %
69	D	43.75 % / 38.54 %
70	A	31.94 % / 38.55 %
71	A	26.39 % / 38.54 %
72	A	8.68 % / 37.85 %
73	D	38.19 % / 38.2 %
74	D	38.89 % / 38.19 %
75	D	46.88 % / 38.54 %
76	A	20.83 % / 38.89 %
77	A	38.19 % / 38.89 %
78	B	26.04 % / 38.89 %
79	C	35.07 % / 38.54 %
80	B	23.26 % / 38.55 %

Q.	Ans.	Correct		Q.	Ans.	Correct		Q.	Ans.	Correct		Q.	Ans.	Correct		Q.	Ans.	Correct
		Skipped				Skipped				Skipped				Skipped				Skipped
81	D	45.49 % 38.54 %		89	C	22.57 % 38.19 %		97	A	36.46 % 38.54 %		105	D	9.72 % 39.24 %		113	A	12.15 % 38.89 %
82	A	32.29 % 38.89 %		90	D	38.19 % 38.55 %		98	C	36.11 % 38.54 %		106	D	28.12 % 39.59 %		114	C	26.39 % 38.54 %
83	A	48.26 % 38.55 %		91	B	38.89 % 38.54 %		99	B	19.44 % 38.55 %		107	A	25.35 % 38.89 %		115	C	21.18 % 38.2 %
84	A	39.24 % 38.19 %		92	B	36.46 % 38.54 %		100	C	47.57 % 38.54 %		108	A	33.33 % 39.59 %		116	B	45.14 % 37.85 %
85	B	47.57 % 38.54 %		93	D	32.29 % 38.54 %		101	D	14.58 % 38.2 %		109	C	38.89 % 39.23 %		117	C	12.15 % 38.54 %
86	A	42.71 % 38.19 %		94	C	43.4 % 37.85 %		102	C	29.86 % 38.89 %		110	C	33.68 % 38.89 %		118	A	37.15 % 37.5 %
87	C	38.54 % 38.2 %		95	B	29.17 % 38.54 %		103	B	16.32 % 38.54 %		111	C	22.92 % 39.23 %		119	A	43.06 % 37.15 %
88	C	28.47 % 38.2 %		96	D	21.53 % 38.54 %		104	D	28.12 % 39.24 %		112	B	20.83 % 38.55 %		120	C	26.04 % 35.42 %

Performance Analysis

Performance Analysis	
Avg. Score (%)	31.0%
Toppers Score (%)	100.0%
Your Score	

//Hints and Solutions//

1. The portion of total deposits of a commercial bank which it has to keep with RBI in the form of cash reserves in termed as CRR. Cash Reserves Ratio (CRR) refers to the proportion of total deposit of the commercial banks which they must keep as reserves with the central bank in the form of cash deposits.

Hence, the correct option is (A).

2. A bank reconciliation statement is a statement prepared by the account holder on a particular date to reconcile the bank balance as per cash book with the balance as per bank passbook or bank statement showing entries causing differences between the two balances.

Bank reconciliation statement is prepared due to the following reason:

1. It brings to light errors that may have committed either in the cash book or passbook.

2. Undue delay in the clearance of cheques deposited is known from the reconciliation.

3. Reconciliation helps the management to verify the accuracy of entries recorded in the cash book.

4. It shows the actual bank balance.

Hence, the correct option is (C).

3. The State Bank of India (SBI) is an Indian multinational, public sector banking and financial services statutory body. It is a government corporation statutory body headquartered in Mumbai, Maharashtra.

Hence, the correct option is (A).

4. RBI has said a sub-target of 8% of net bank credit, or credit equivalent amount of off-balance sheet exposure, whichever is higher, shall become applicable for foreign banks with 20 branches and above, for lending to MSMEs from FY19.

For foreign Bank, priority sector lending targets are 32% of net banking credit.

Hence, the correct option is (A).

5. PMLA stipulates that records pertaining to all cash transactions greater than Rs. 10 lakhs, all integrally connected series of transactions are maintained for a period of 10 years. Prevention of Money Laundering Act, 2002 is an Act of the Parliament of India enacted by the NDA government to prevent money-laundering and to provide for confiscation of property derived from money-laundering. PMLA and the Rules notified there under came into force with effect from July 1, 2005.

Hence, the correct option is (B).

6. There are certain transactions that require more clarity or there are some errors that are not rectified before the finalization of accounts. All such entries are parked in a temporary account known as a suspense account.

The suspense account will be shown in the balance sheet either on the asset side or liabilities side, depending on the balance of the suspense account.

Hence, the correct option is (D).

7. Real-Time Gross Settlement (RTGS) is management by Reserve Bank of India. Real-time gross settlements are a process that is used for high-value inter-bank transactions. These transactions typically need instant and full clearing and are generally done by the central bank of the country.

Hence, the correct option is (B).

8. When depreciation is recorded to provision for depreciation account the asset appears at original cost. Depreciation is accumulated as provision on the liability side of balance sheet and when it is actually charged on an asset at that time depreciation is subtracted from asset cost.

Hence, the correct option is (A).

9. Factors responsible for creating conditions for the emergence and growth of monopoly are control over strategic raw materials, patent rights, and government licensing. A firm enjoys a monopoly when it is the sole seller of its product and the product has no close substitutes. The fundamental cause of monopoly is the barrier to entry.

Control over strategic raw materials- It is important to start thinking about control strategy for raw materials during early development and as product knowledge evolves. It is imperative that the rationale for having a specific control strategy for excipients should be driven through risk assessment.

Government licensing- It means that before a firm can enter an industry, it needs to take permission from the government. Licensing is used to ensure minimum standards of competency. By not granting licenses to new firms, the government aims to assure that only one firm operates in the market.

Patent Rights- Certain big private companies are engaged in research and development activities. At times, they come up with new products or new technologies. As a reward for their risk and investment in research, the government grants them patent rights. The period for which patent rights are granted is known as patent life.

Hence, the correct option is (D).

10. In the case of inferior goods, the income effect partially offsets the substitution effect. When the price of an inferior good falls, its negative income effect will tend to reduce the quantity purchased, while the substitution effect will tend to increase the quantity purchased.

The income effect describes how the change in the price of a good can change the quantity that consumers will demand of that good and related goods, based on how the price change affects their real income.

The change in the quantity demanded resulting from a change in the price of a good can vary depending on the interaction of the income and substitution effects.

For inferior goods, the income effect dominates the substitution effect and leads consumers to purchase more of a good, and less of substitute goods, when the price rises.

Hence, the correct option is (A).

11. A duopoly is a form of oligopoly, where only two companies dominate the market. The companies in a duopoly tend to compete against one another, reducing the chance of monopolistic market power.

- A small collection of firms who dominate a market is called an oligopoly. A duopoly is a special case of an oligopoly, in which only two firms exist.

- The two firms produce homogeneous and indistinguishable goods.

- There are no other firms in the market who produce the same or substitute goods.

- No other firms can or will enter the market.

- Collusive behaviour is prohibited. Firms cannot act together to form a cartel.

- There exists one market for produced goods.

Hence, the correct option is (C).

12. Value maximization is essentially the core of the neoclassical firm theory. It says that all firms do or should seek to maximize their total market value, and maximizing social welfare as a result.

The self-serving leader tends to focus on their own needs and challenges more than those of their team's. Value maximization theory fails to address the problem of self-serving management. Instead of aiming to support and develop their teams, their mindset turns to one of self-interest and self-preservation.

Hence, the correct option is (A).

13. The selling cost is incurred in the case of monopolistic competition because the firms are interested in promoting their products by various methods of advertising and marketing. The selling costs are part of the promotion of the product for enticing the end-users.

Hence, the correct option is (B).

14. Oligopoly is a market structure with a small number of firms, none of which can keep the others from having significant influence. The concentration ratio measures the market share of the largest firms. A monopoly is one firm, a duopoly is two firms and an oligopoly is two or more firms.

Monopolistic competition is a type of imperfect competition such that there are many producers competing against each other, but selling products that are differentiated from one another and hence are not perfect substitutes.

A monopoly exists when a specific person or enterprise is the only supplier of a particular commodity.

Hence, the correct option is (D).

15. In microeconomics, the Bertrand-Edgeworth model of price-setting oligopoly looks at what happens when there is a homogeneous product (i.e. consumers want to buy from the cheapest seller) where there is a limit to the output of firms which they are willing and able to sell at a particular price.

This process continues indefinitely and the price keeps moving up and down between OP_1 and OP_2 Obviously, according to Edgeworth's model of duopoly, equilibrium is unstable and indeterminate since price and output are never determined.

Hence, the correct option is (A).

16. The abolition of industrial licensing, dismantling of price controls, dilution of reservations for small-scale industries and the virtual abolition of the monopolies law, relaxation of restrictions on foreign investment, lowering of corporate and personal tax rates, removal of restrictions on managerial remuneration, etc.

Hence, the correct option is (D).

17. A monopolistic trade practise is deemed to be prejudicial to public interest except when Authorized by Central Government. to give effect to the terms of any agreement to which the Central Government is a party, by written order, permits the owner of any undertaking to carry on any such trade practice.

Hence, the correct option is (A).

18. Sale of Business is not a method of privatization. Privatization is a method of transfer or sale of public assets to private ownership. One of the important methods of privatization is either disinvestment or privatization of ownership, through the sale of equity. Privatization can be defined as a process of transferring ownership or management of an enterprise from the public sector to the private sector. It helps to increase the size and dynamism of the private sector. It also helps to reduce administrative burdens on the public sector.

Hence, the correct option is (C).

19. The pre-liberalisation era of Indian Economy was under the grip of the unfavourable and alarming balance of payment. This era began at the time of independence in 1947 and lasted till the introduction of New Economic Policy in 1991 by Dr Manmohan Singh, the Union finance minister of India. This era is marked by the emergence and growth of popular 'Nehru Model' of development. It was initiated in 1991 with the goal of making the economy more market- and service-oriented, and expanding the role of private and foreign investment and to eradicate the unfavourable and alarming balance of payments.

Hence, the correct option is (D).

20. Conditions for the success of privatization:-

- The commitment of political leadership.

- There must be a multiplicity of private suppliers for the benefit of competition to follow.

- Freedom of entry to provide goods and services.

- The business organization has no control over money and capital market, hence it is not an element of the internal environment.

Hence, the correct option is (B).

21. Privatization of ownership through the sale of equity shares is called disinvestment. Disinvestment is aimed at reducing the financial burden on the government due to inefficient PSUs and

to improve public finances. It introduces competition and market discipline and helps to depoliticize non-essential services.

Hence, the correct option is (B).

22. Any practice which indicates misuse of one's power to abuse the market in terms of production and sales of goods and services was defined as monopolistic trade practice. The objective of such practices is to eliminate competition, take advantage of monopoly and charge unreasonably high prices.

A manufacturing company that has only one product has established the following standards for its variable manufacturing overhead. Variable manufacturing overhead standards are based on machine-hours. Standard hours per unit of output 4.50 machine-hours Standard variable overhead rate $11.52 per machine-hour.

Hence, the correct option is (B).

23. Industrial Policy Resolution of 1956 (IPR 1956) is a resolution adopted by the Indian Parliament in April 1956. It was the first comprehensive statement on the industrial development of India. The 1956 policy continued to constitute the basic economic policy for a long time.

Hence, the correct option is (C).

24. Planning is the function of management that involves setting objectives and determining a course of action for achieving those objectives. Planning requires that managers be aware of environmental conditions facing their organization and forecast future conditions. Planning is a process consisting of several steps.

Hence, the correct option is (A).

25. A subordinate should have only one superior to whom he or she is directly responsible is known as Unity of command implies that a sub-ordinate should receive orders & instructions from only one boss. It means one head, one plan for a group of activities having similar objectives.

Hence, the correct option is (C).

26. Inline and staff organization, the staff performs the function of advising management. A "line function" is one that directly advances an organization in its core work. This always includes production and sales, and sometimes also marketing. A "staff function" supports the organization with specialized advisory and support functions.

Hence, the correct option is (B).

27. In a business organization, it is done at each level of the organization, top, middle, and lower management. The top management level makes long-term plans, middle management level make departmental plans and lower management level makes operating plans.

Hence, the correct option is (A).

28. Effective supervision is one who offers leadership, resolves conflicts, and provides an ear for their team. This is a person who can recognize their own emotion in a situation, recognize the emotions of others, is empathetic, and has top-notch social skills.

Hence, the correct option is (A).

29. Leadership is a function of all the following except product or service. Leadership can be defined as a process of influencing the behaviour of people at work towards the realization of a specific goal. The influence under leadership is always for the achievement of a common goal.

Hence, the correct option is (B).

30. The planning function is conducted at all three levels.

Top-level Plans: Plans which are formulated by general managers and directors are called top-level plans. Under these plans, the objectives, budget, policies etc. for the whole organization are laid down. These plans are mostly long term plans.

Middle-level Plans: Managerial hierarchy at the middle level includes the departmental managers. A corporate has many departments like purchase department, sales department, finance department, personnel department etc. The plans formulated by the departmental managers are called middle-level plans.

Lower level Plans: These plans are prepared by the foreman or the supervisors. They take the existence of the actual workplace and the problems connected with it. They are formulated for a short period of time and called short term plans.

Hence, the correct option is (B).

31. The functions are key to management at all levels, from the entry positions to higher roles of management. Furthermore, every five functions – Planning, Organizing, Staffing, Directing, and Control and Coordination are linked to each other.

Management comprises planning, organizing, staffing, leading, directing, and controlling an organization (a group of one or more people or entities) or effort for the purpose of accomplishing a goal. One of the most important duties of a manager is effectively using an organization's resources.

Hence, the correct option is (B).

32. The process of recording transactions in different journals is called journalizing. Journalizing is the process of recording a business transaction in the accounting records. This activity only applies to the double-entry bookkeeping system.

Journalizing in accounting is the system by which all business transactions are recorded for your financial records. A business transaction is first recorded in a journal, also called a Book of Original Entry. Adding new journal entries is called journalizing.

Hence, the correct option is (D).

33. The minimum and maximum values for the correlation coefficient depend on the distributions of the random variables. These values are in [-1,1] although, it is possible to have a larger minimum (smaller maximum) value for correlation coefficient than -1 (1), depending on the distributions.

(Here correlation coefficient refers to the Pearson Correlation Coefficient.)

Hence, the correct option is (C).

34. Files held on a storage device are identified by a special block of data held as the first block on the file. This block is called a file label.

A block is the smallest readable or writable unit that can be addressed. The size of these blocks varies. Block sizes of 512 Bytes used to be standard. The block size used in a file system directly impacts the maximum size of the file system e.g. with a 4K block size an ext2, ext3, or NTFS file system can reach 16TB.

Block storage, sometimes referred to as block-level storage, is a technology that is used to store data files on Storage Area Networks (SANs) or cloud-based storage environments. Block storage breaks up data into blocks and then stores those blocks as separate pieces, each with a unique identifier.

Hence, the correct option is (A).

35. A Management Information System (MIS) is a computer system consisting of hardware and software that serves as the backbone of an organization's operations. An MIS gathers data from multiple online systems, analyzes the information, and reports data to aid in management decision-making.

Hence, the correct option is (A).

36. We know that a positive relationship between two variables with an upward-sloping curve. We illustrate a linear relationship with a curve whose slope is constant a nonlinear relationship is illustrated with a curve whose slope changes.

Hence, the correct option is (A).

37. The Horizontal curve represents the value of the coefficient of correlation to be zero. A horizontal line has r = 0. This means that there is no relationship between the two variables and the Y values are just randomly scattered on the grid.

Hence, the correct option is (C).

38.

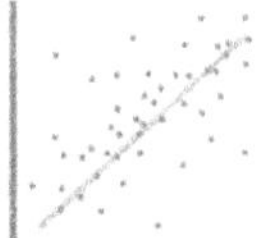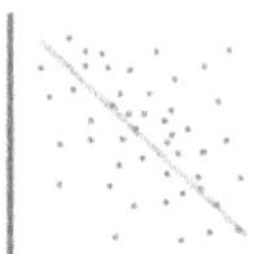

If the correlation coefficient of the two variables is 0, it signifies that there is no linear relationship between the variables. When the value of ρ is close to 0, generally between -0.1 and +0.1, the variables are said to have no linear relationship or a very weak linear relationship.

Hence, the correct option is (D).

39. The sale of a business asset on credit is recorded in a sales journal. The sales journal is also totalled periodically and this total is credited to sales account in the ledger. The sales journal is used to record all of the company sales on credit. Most often these sales are made up of inventory sales or other merchandise sales.

Hence, the correct option is (B).

40. Pearson's Coefficient of Correlation is an extensively used mathematical method in which the numerical representation is applied to measure the level of relation between linear related variables. The coefficient of correlation is expressed by "r".

Hence, the correct option is (B).

41. Apart from the investment in fixed assets, every business organisation needs to invest in current assets. This investment facilitates the smooth day-to-day operations of the business. Insufficient investment in current assets may make it more difficult for an organisation to meet its payment obligations.

Net Working Capital = CA - CL i.e Current assets-Current Liabilities

Current assets keep revolving or circulating fast, the temporary working capital is also called revolving capital.

Hence, the correct option is (B).

42. To calculate the cost of debt, a company must determine the total amount of interest it is paying on each of its debts for the year. Then it divides this number by the total of all of its debt. The result is the cost of debt. The cost of debt formula is the effective interest rate multiplied by (1 - tax rate).

Hence, the correct option is (B).

43. The matching approach is a strategy of working capital financing where the short-term funds are sourced from short-term debts and long-term from long-term debts. Structural ratios are a type of capital structure ratios that are based on the proportions of debt and equity in the capital structure of the firm. The Economic Order Quantity (EOQ) is a part of inventory management. It is the ideal ordering quantity which minimizes total holding and ordering costs of the year. Use of Bonus share is an integral part of the dividend policy of a firm.

Hence, the correct option is (C).

44. The Gordon Growth Model (GGM) is used to determine the intrinsic value of a stock based on a future series of dividends that grow at a constant rate. It is a popular and straightforward variant of a dividend discount model (DDM).

Hence, the correct option is (B).

45. The accounting rate of return, also known as the simple or average rate of return, measures the amount of profit or return expected on an investment. ARR does not consider the time value of money or cash flows which can be an integral part of maintaining a business.

Hence, the correct option is (A).

46. It is calculated by dividing the annual dividend per share by market value per share. The ratio is generally expressed in percentage form and is sometimes called dividend yield percentage.

Hence, the correct option is (A).

47. Current Ratio = $\dfrac{Current\ Assets\ (C.A)}{Current\ Liabilities\ (C.L)}$ (C.L) = $\dfrac{2}{1}$ So,

$$CA = 2\,CL$$

Now, Working Capital = Current Assets(C.A) — Current Liabilities (C.L) $= Rs.\,60,000$

So, $C.A - C.L = 60,000$

$2\,CL - CL = 60,000$

C.L = $Rs.\,60,000$

Now, $C.A = 2 \times 60,000 = Rs.\,1,20,000$

Hence, the correct option is (C).

48. The capital budgeting process consists of five steps:

1. Identify and evaluate potential opportunities

2. Estimate operating and implementation costs

3. Estimate cash flow or benefit

4. Assess risk

5. Implement

Hence, the correct option is (B).

49. Feedback and counseling discuss the steps the employee can take for improvement, provide support, and give critical and supportive feedback. It includes critical as well as positive comments, which are given with skill and sensitivity.

Hence, the correct option is (D).

50. Fixed assets are not readily liquid and cannot be easily converted into cash. They are not sold or consumed by a company. Instead, the asset is used to produce goods and services.

Most tangible assets, such as buildings, machinery, and equipment, can be depreciated.

Hence, the correct option is (C).

51. The concept of Human relations was developed by Elton Mayo. In the 1920s, Elton Mayo, an Australian-born psychologist and organizational theorist, began his research on the behaviour of people in groups and how it affects individuals in the workplace, known as the Hawthorne studies.

Hence, the correct option is (C).

52. Human resource management is concerned with all employees. It is designed to maximize employee performance in the service of an employer's strategic objectives. Human resource management is primarily concerned with the management of people within organizations, focusing on policies and systems.

Hence, the correct option is (D).

53. The portion of the acquisition cost of an asset yet to be allocated is known as written down value. Written-down value is the value of an asset after accounting for depreciation or amortization.

Hence, the correct option is (A).

54. Dividends are paid on the paid-up-capital. Paid-up-Capital is the money actually received by the company against the shares sold. Hence, the dividends are paid only to those shareholders who have paid money.

Hence, the correct option is (C).

55. 1) In the production mechanism, it is not necessary to allow the major share of total productive gains/output to labor, which is a factor of production. Instead, labor is provided wages in exchange for their services. Thus, Assertion {A} is false.

2) Strike refers to a situation when employees of a firm/industry partially or completely stop working for a short period of time.

Hence, the correct option is (B).

56. The objectives of the training is increased morale, increased productivity, and favourable reaction to change. Training is a process of enhancing the skills, knowledge, competencies of employees so that they can perform present jobs.

Hence, the correct option is (D).

57. The present value is equivalent to the principal amount. Present value is the concept that states an amount of money today is worth more than that same amount in the future. In other words, money received in the future is not worth as much as an equal amount received today. Receiving $1,000 today is worth more than $1,000 five years from now.

Hence, the correct option is (B).

58. A promotion mix is a particular combination of promotional tools used by a company to communicate with its audiences. It refers to all the decisions related to the promotion of sales of products and services.

Hence, the correct option is (A).

59. Green marketing is the marketing of products that are presumed to be environmentally safe. It incorporates a broad range of activities, including product modification, changes to the production process, sustainable packaging, as well as modifying advertising.

Hence, the correct option is (D).

60. A negotiable instrument can be transferred from one person to another by a simple process. In the case of bearer instruments, simple delivery to the transferee is sufficient. In the case of an order instrument, two things are required for a valid transfer: endorsement or signature of the holder and delivery.

Hence, the correct option is (A).

61. There are seven main types of internet marketing:

- Social media marketing.
- Online marketing.
- Affiliate marketing.
- E-mail marketing.
- Internet advertising.
- Search engine optimization (SEO).
- Paid advertising.

Product Mix and Branding is not a form of Internet Marketing.

Hence, the correct option is (D).

62. When the consignee receives the goods, it is recorded as "inward consignment" in his books. Consignee gets commission for his services from the consignor. He usually recovers from the consignor all the expenses incurred by him on consignment.

Hence, the correct option is (D).

63. Problems of marketing communication are-

- Problem 1: Inexperience or Understaffed.
- Problem 2: New Marketing Trends.
- Problem 3: Interpreting marketing report data.
- Problem 4: Lack of Communication.
- Problem 5: Closing the Sales Loop.

Hence, the correct option is (D).

64. The marketing manager has to carry out their responsibilities integrating all these factors in the management process. Responsible for managing the company's marketing initiatives. Uses market research and analysis to direct marketing strategy and planning. Oversees the production of all promotional materials and marketing campaigns. Reports marketing and sales results to senior executives.

Hence, the correct option is (A).

65. Sales promotion includes all promotional activities other than advertising, personal selling, and publicity. American Marketing Association, "sales promotion refers to those marketing activities, other than personal selling, advertising, and publicity that stimulate consumer purchasing and dealer effectiveness, such as displays, shows, and exhibitions, demonstrations.

Hence, the correct option is (A).

66. Every business transaction affects at least two accounts, our accounting system is known as a double-entry system. The double-entry system of accounting is based on the dual aspect concept. The dual aspect concept defines that every transaction gives two effects or every business transaction affects at least two accounts. One in debit and another in credit side.

For example, Goods purchases for cash of Rs. 2000 in this transaction, two accounts i.e. cash and purchases are affected. Cash and purchases are both real accounts. The rule for a real account is "debit what comes in and credit what goes out". Accordingly, in this transaction, goods are coming into the business, and against that cash is going out.

Hence, the correct option is (B).

67. Philip Kotler in 1972 said that "Marketing is the set of human activities directed at facilitating and consummating exchanges". It means that marketing management is the analysis, planning, implementation, and control of programs designed to bring about desired exchanges with target audiences for the purpose of personal or mutual gain.

Hence, the correct option is (A).

68. The factors affecting pricing decisions are varied and multiple. Basically, the prices of products and services are determined by the interplay of five factors, demand and supply conditions, production and associated costs, competition, buyer's bargaining power, and the perceived value.

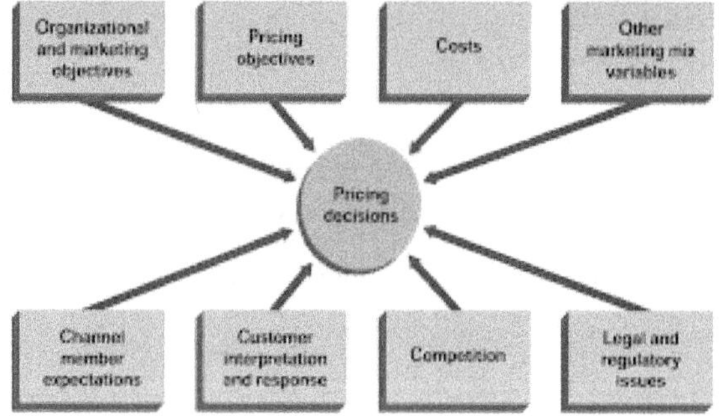

Hence, the correct option is (D).

69. Product Planning is the ongoing process of identifying and articulating market requirements that define a product's feature set. Additionally, a small company must have an exit strategy for its product in case the product does not sell.

Co-ordination of New Product Planning and Development

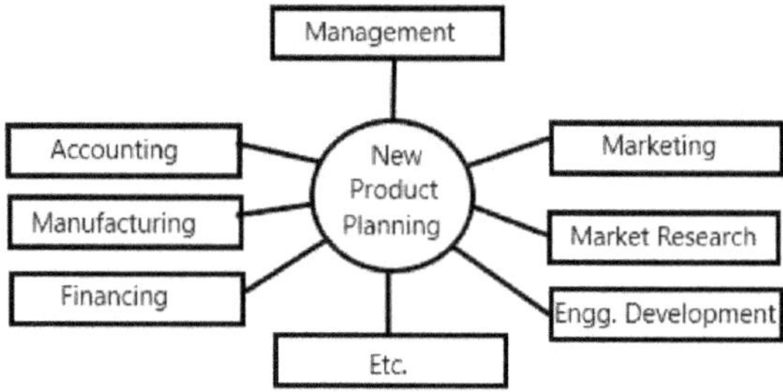

Hence, the correct option is (D).

70. The degree of financial leverage (DFL) measures the percentage change in EPS for a unit change in operating income, also known as earnings before interest and taxes (EBIT). This ratio indicates that the higher the degree of financial leverage, the more volatile earnings will be.

Hence, the correct option is (A).

71. The internet offers marketers a fast, versatile, and inexpensive is known communication medium. In the communication process, a medium is a channel or system of communication + the means by which information (the message) is transmitted between a speaker or writer (the sender) and an audience (the receiver). The plural form is media, and the term is also known as a channel.

Hence, the correct option is (A).

72. The concept of the marketing mix involves the deliberate and careful choice of organisation product, price, promotion and place strategies and policies. A policy is a deliberate system of principles to guide decisions and achieve rational outcomes. A policy is a statement of intent and is implemented as a procedure or protocol. Policies are generally adopted by a governance body within an organization.

Hence, the correct option is (A).

73. Pricing objectives are a combination of product line promotion, cash Recovery, and Profit Maximisation.

It involves:

1) marketing, and strategic objectives of the company.

2) the objectives of your product or brand.

3) consumer price elasticity and price points.

4) the resources you have available.

Hence, the correct option is (D).

74. The marketing programme is part of pre-planning. It is the programme of marketing efforts in which decisions are taken. The following factors affect the planning of marketing programme are:-

1.Marketing Strategy- A marketing strategy refers to a business's overall game plan for reaching prospective consumers and turning them into customers of the products or services the business provides.

2. Marketing Mix- The marketing mix has been defined as the "set of marketing tools that the firm uses to pursue its marketing objectives in the target market". Thus the marketing mix refers to four broad levels of marketing decision: product, price, place, and promotion.

3. Demand Variable- The quantity demanded is a function of five factors- price, buyer income, the price of related goods, consumer tastes, and any consumer expectations of future supply and price. As these factors change, so too does the quantity demanded.

Hence, the correct option is (D).

75. A product line strategy is a coherent approach to advance related products. It guides managers to improve the performance of their products and services, and to avoid disjointed actions and investments. A good strategy will respond to change, whether major disruptions or incremental.

For example, a cosmetic company that's already selling a high-priced product line of makeup (that might include foundation, eyeliner, mascara, and lipstick) under one of its well-known brands might launch a product line under the same brand name but at a lower price point.

Hence, the correct option is (D).

76. The principal function of an electronic market is to facilitate the search for the required product or service. Airline booking systems are example of the electronic market.

Hence, the correct option is (A).

77. Depreciation is a decline in the value of tangible fixed assets. Depreciation is the permanent and continuous decrease in the book value of a depreciable fixed asset due to use, effluxion of time, obsolescence, expiration of legal rights or any other cause.

Hence, the correct option is (A).

78. Discount allowed is a kind of deduction from account receivable. Equity ratio higher is the protection to creditors. Creditors usually like a low debt to equity ratio because a low ratio (less than 1) is the indication of greater protection to their money. Discount allowed is a concession that is given to the customers in respect of the amount receivable from them for the sales done. When a discount is given, it reduces the total receivable amount to the extent of the discount amount.

Hence, the correct option is (B).

79. Market Arbitrage is basically buying a security in one market and simultaneously selling it in another market at a higher price, thereby profiting from the temporary difference in prices.

Market Arbitrage is, in theory, considered to be a riskless activity because traders are simply buying and selling equal amounts of the same asset at the same time.

Hence, the correct option is (C).

80. When the required rate of return is more than the coupon rate, then bonds will sell at discount. If the investor's required rate of return is above the coupon interest rate, the bond will sell at a discount (below par value), but if the investor's required rate of return is below the coupon interest rate, the bond will sell at a price above its par value.

Hence, the correct option is (B).

81. Depreciation is an accounting method of allocating the cost of a tangible or physical asset over its useful life or life expectancy. Depreciation represents how much of an asset's value has been used up. The following factors that affect the computation of depreciation.

1. Cost and Residual Value- The residual value of an asset is the estimated amount that an asset's owner would earn by disposing of the asset, less any disposal cost. With residual value, it's assumed that the asset has reached the end of its useful life.

2. Estimated useful life- Useful life is the estimated lifespan of a depreciable fixed asset, during which it can be expected to contribute to company operations. This is an important concept in accounting since a fixed asset is depreciated over its useful life.

3.Method of depreciation- There are four methods for depreciation, straight line, declining balance, the sum of the years' digits, and units of production.

a. Straight-line basis is a method of calculating depreciation and amortization, the process of expensing an asset over a longer period of time.

b. Declining balance- The declining balance method is an accelerated depreciation system of recording larger depreciation expenses during the earlier years of an asset's useful life and recording smaller depreciation expenses during the asset's later years.

c. Sum of the years' digits- the sum of the years' digits is an accelerated method for determining an asset's expected depreciation over time.

d. Units of production depreciation- Depreciation expense for a given year is calculated by dividing the original cost of the equipment less its salvage value, by the expected number of units the asset should produce given its useful life.

Hence, the correct option is (D).

82. Discount allowed is the expense of the business. A discount allowed is when the seller of goods or services grants a payment discount to a buyer.

Hence, the correct option is (A).

83. Current assets are short-term assets that can be converted into cash on a need basis. Current assets may consist of inventory, debtors, bills receivables, cash on hand, bank balance, etc.

Hence, the correct option is (A).

84. Drawings accounts will be debited if the business's owner withdraws cash from the business for personal use. Goods withdrawn for personal use by the owner of a business reduce inventory and are recorded on a drawings account.

Hence, the correct option is (A).

85. RTGS stands for Real Time Gross Settlement, which can be explained as a system where there is continuous and real-time settlement of fund-transfers, individually on a transaction by transaction basis (without netting).

Hence, the correct option is (B).

86. Bill discounting is an arrangement whereby the seller recovers an amount of sales bill from the financial intermediaries before it is due. Such intermediaries charge a fee for the service.

Hence, the correct option is (A).

87. The business entity concept states that the transactions associated with a business must be separately recorded from those of its owners or other businesses.

There are many types of business entities, such as sole proprietorships, partnerships, corporations, and government entities.

There are a number of reasons for the business entity concept, including:

- Each business entity is taxed separately.
- It is needed to calculate the financial performance and financial position of an entity.
- It is needed when an organization is liquidated, to determine the amounts of payouts to the various owners.
- It is needed from a liability perspective, to ascertain the assets available in the event of a legal judgment against a business entity.
- It is not possible to audit the records of a business if the records have been combined with those of other entities and/or individuals.

Hence, the correct option is (C).

88. An ESOP (Employee stock ownership plan) refers to an employee benefit plan which offers employees an ownership interest in the organization. An organization grants ESOPs to its employees for buying a specified number of shares of the company at a defined price after the option period (a certain number of years). Before an employee could exercise his option, he needs to go through the pre-defined vesting period which implies that the employee has to work for the organization until a part or the entire stock options could be exercised.

Hence, the correct option is (C).

89. Discount for quick repayment of debt is normally referred to as cash discount. It is called cash discount which might be offered or received.

Hence, the correct option is (C).

90. Operating profit reflects the profitability of a company's operations. Operating profit is also referred to as earnings before interest and tax (EBIT).

Hence, the correct option is (D).

91. The sales journal is used to record all of the company sales on credit. Most often these sales are made up of inventory sales or other merchandise sales.

Hence, the correct option is (B).

92. Trial Balance is a statement. A trial balance is a list of all the general ledger accounts contained in the ledger of a business. This list will contain the name of each nominal ledger account and the value of that nominal ledger balance. Each nominal ledger account will hold either a debit balance or a credit balance.

Hence, the correct option is (B).

93. Sales and purchase journal doesn't record cash sales and purchases made against cash. It is where the seller receives the cash consideration at the time of delivery and the purchase used in the periodic inventory system to record the purchases of merchandise for resale. This account reports the gross amount of purchases of merchandise. Therefore, the sales and purchase journal doesn't record cash sales and purchases.

Hence, the correct option is (D).

94. Cash received from the debtor is recorded in the cash receipts journal. The cash receipts journal is a special journal used to record cash received by a business.

Hence, the correct option is (C).

95. Salary Account is nominal Account. Accounts that are related to expenses, losses, incomes, or gains are called nominal accounts.

Hence, the correct option is (B).

96. Cash purchases are recorded in the cash payments journal. A cash payment journal or cash disbursement journal is used to record all cash payments made by the business.

Hence, the correct option is (D).

97. A brief explanation recorded below every entry in the General Journal is commonly known as narration. A short explanation of each transaction is written under each entry which is called narration.

Hence, the correct option is (A).

98. The purchase of plant and machinery is an example of capital expenditure.

It is a payment for goods or services recorded or capitalized on the balance sheet instead of expensed on the income statement. Capital expenditure spending is important for companies to maintain existing property and equipment, and invest in new technology and other assets for growth.

Hence, the correct option is (C).

99. A credit note is a basis for recording a transaction in a sales return journal. A credit note or credit memo is a commercial document issued by a seller to a buyer.

Hence, the correct option is (B).

100. Transferring entries from journal to ledger account is commonly known as posting. Posting refers to the process of transferring entries in the journal into the accounts in the ledger. Posting to the ledger is the classifying phase of accounting.

Hence, the correct option is (C).

101. If wages are paid for the construction of business premises cash account is credited and premises account is debited. If wages are paid for the construction of business premises the number of wages will be debited to the premises account because, according to IFRS, any expense that brings the asset to use or brings the asset in existence should be added to the cost of that machinery. A cash account is credited because cash is being paid for incurring the wages.

Hence, the correct option is (D).

102. Human resources will not appear in the balance sheet according to the money measurement concept. The value of human resources is generally not shown in the balance sheet as per the money measurement concept. The money measurement concept means only those transactions will be recorded in the books of accounts which can be measured in monetary terms. Accounting ignores the qualitative aspects it records only quantitative aspects.

Hence, the correct option is (C).

103. The provision for doubtful debts is the estimated amount of bad debt. that will arise from accounts receivable that have been issued but not yet collected. Later, when you identify a specific customer invoice that is not going to be paid, eliminate it against the provision for doubtful debts.

In other words, the amount of the provision for a discount is calculated after deducting bad debts and provision for doubtful debts. from sundry debtors. Suppose, sundry debtors total Rs. 20, 000 provisions for doubtful debts is required at 5% and provision for discounts at $2\frac{1}{2}$ %.

Hence, the correct option is (B).

104. Sales Account is not a Real Account. As it comes in the trading account of final accounts, it is considered that sales & purchases are nominal accounts.

Hence, the correct option is (C).

105. Value of goods withdrawn by the proprietor for his personal use should be credited to purchases account. The goods taken by the proprietor for personal use reduces the inventory of the business. Hence, it is placed on a temporary drawings account. It reduces the Owner's equity account.

Hence, the correct option is (D).

106. Outstanding expenses which are liability account must be recorded in the accounting period if they relate to the accounting year. An Outstanding expense is an expense which is due but has not been paid. An expense becomes outstanding when the company has taken the benefit, but the related payment has not been made. Outstanding expenses appear within the current liability section of the balance sheet.

Hence, the correct option is (D).

107. M/s Stationery Mart will debit the purchase of stationery to purchases account. The stationery is the stock of the firm so it's not considered as general expenses or stationery. A general and administrative expense (G&A) refers to expenditures related to the day-to-day operations of a business. In the company's income statement, these expenses generally appear under operating expenses.

Hence, the correct option is (A).

108. Small items like pencils, pens, files, etc. are written off within a year according to materiality concept. Materiality is a concept or convention within auditing and accounting relating to the important significance of an amount, transaction, or discrepancy.

Hence, the correct option is (A).

109. The business enterprise is separate from its owner according to entity concept. The concept of a business entity assumes that a business has a distinct and separate entity from its owners. It means that for the purposes of accounting, the business and its owners are to be treated as two separate entities. Keeping this in view, when a person brings in some money as capital into his business, in accounting records, it is treated as a liability of the business to the owner.

Here, one separate entity (owner) is assumed to be giving money to another distinct entity (business unit).

Similarly, when the owner withdraws any money from the business for his personal expenses(drawings), it is treated as a reduction of the owner's capital and consequently a reduction in the liabilities of the business.

Hence, the correct option is (C).

110. The policy to anticipate no profit and provide for all possible losses arise due to the concept of conservatism. The concept of conservatism (also called 'prudence') provides guidance for recording transactions in the book of accounts and is based on the policy of playing safe. The concept states that a conscious approach should be adopted in ascertaining income so that the profits of the enterprise are not overstated.

The concept of conservatism requires that profits should not be recorded until realized but all losses, even those which may have a remote possibility, are to be provided in the books of accounts.

Hence, the correct option is (C).

111. According to the entity concept, the proprietor pays interest on drawings. If the proprietor has drawn funds from the business, then it will be treated as a loan to the proprietor by the firm, company, business and therefore Interest is charged from the proprietor. Such Interest is the income of the entity and thus, is credited to the account of the entity.

Hence, the correct option is (C).

112. The cost concept basically recognises historical cost or the acquisition cost of the asset. The value of an asset is to be determined on the basis of historical cost.

Hence, the correct option is (B).

113. If the Market value of closing inventory is less than its cost price, inventory will be shown at a marketable value. When the market value of closing inventory is less than the opening inventory it means that the business has undergone loss and its effect will be shown at the credit side of the book of entry. This shows that on that financial year the business recorded loss and the amount of the loss that was incurred should be quoted for proper accountability of income.

Hence, the correct option is (A).

114. The realization principle is the concept that revenue can only be recognized once the underlying goods or services associated with the revenue have been delivered or rendered, respectively. Thus, revenue can only be recognized after it has been earned.

Hence, the correct option is (C).

115. The timeliness concept states that the publication or presentation of financial statements should not be delayed. The timeliness principle in accounting refers to the need for accounting information to be presented to the users in time to fulfill their decision making needs.

Hence, the correct option is (C).

116. Accounting Standards are written policy document issued by expert accounting body or by government or regulatory body covering the aspects of recognition, treatment, measurement, presentation and disclosure of accounting transaction and events in the financial statements.

Accounting Standards (ASs) provide a framework and standard accounting policies so that financial statements of different enterprises become comparable.

The Accounting Standards seek to ensure that the financial statements of an enterprise should give a true and fair view of its financial position and working results.

The Accounting Standards not only prescribe appropriate accounting treatment of complex business transactions but also foster greater transparency and market discipline.

Hence, the correct option is (B).

117. Accountancy is the practice of recording, classifying, and reporting on business transactions for a business. It provides feedback to management regarding the financial results and status of an organization.

Hence, the correct option is (C).

118. "Debit the receiver, and credit the giver" is a golden rule for a personal account. Personal accounts are the accounts for individual, firms, companies etc. By debit the receiver means the person who is receiving goods on credit will be debited and the person who is giving will be credited.

Hence, the correct option is (A).

119. A cash account is a real account. A real account is a general ledger account that does not close at the end of the accounting year. In other words, the balances in the real accounts are carried over to become the beginning balances of the next accounting period.

Hence, the correct option is (A).

120. Sales + Gross Profit = Revenue

Gross profit is the profit a company makes after deducting the costs associated with making and selling its products, or the costs associated with providing its services. Gross profit will appear on a company's income statement and can be calculated by subtracting the cost of goods sold (COGS) from revenue (sales).

Hence, the correct option is (C).

Q.1 The demand curve is related to _________.

A. Price
B. Quantity
C. Both (A) and (B)
D. None of these

Q.2 Market with one buyer and one seller is called _____.

A. Monopsony
B. Monopoly
C. Bilateral Monopoly
D. None of the above

Q.3 Land on lease should be shown in the balance sheet contrary to the fact that the company does not own that piece of land is the implementation of which accounting concept?

A. Matching concept
B. Accrual concept
C. Prudence concept
D. Substance over form concept

Q.4 Which of the following is an important dynamic variable?

A. Superior's style and behaviour
B. Organisational nature
C. The task structure
D. Cultural variables

Q.5 How many sellers are present in duopoly?

A. 1
B. 2
C. 3
D. 4

Q.6 Depreciation is charged on fixed assets to comply with which of the following accounting principle?

A. Matching concept
B. Prudence concept
C. Timeliness concept
D. Reliability concept

Q.7 Net profit is computed in which of the following?

A. Balance sheet
B. Income statement
C. Cash flow statement
D. Statement of changes in equity

Q.8 Education cess is leviable in case of _________.

A. An individual and HUF
B. A company assessee only
C. All assesses
D. None of the above

Q.9 Deduction under section 40(B) shall be allowed on account of salary/remuneration paid to _______.

A. Any partner
B. Major partner only
C. Working partner only
D. None of the above

Q.10 Which of the following financial statements shows the financial position of a business at a specific date?

A. Balance sheet
B. Income statement
C. Cash flow statement
D. Statement of changes in equity

Q.11 Business loss can be set off against salary income.

A. True
B. False
C. It cannot be said with certainty
D. It is decided by the Assessing Officer

Q.12 Guarantee for the employer for the loss out of employees dishonest is _________.

A. Burglary insurance
B. Fidelity insurance
C. Third-party insurance
D. Medical insurance

Q.13 Annual report on currency and finance is published by _________.

A. SIDBI
B. Reserve Bank of India
C. Ministry of finance
D. None of the above

Q.14 SEZ policy in India is motivated by the experience of ______.

A. Japan
B. China
C. USA
D. Germany

Q.15 In order to control credit

A. CRR should be increased and Bank Rate should be decreased
B. CRR should be decreased and Bank Rate should be decreased
C. CRR and Bank Rate should be increased
D. CRR should be decreased and Bank Rate should be increased

Q.16 Total number of RRBs now functioning is _________.

A. 84
B. 43
C. 112
D. 154

Q.17 Which of the following provides financial aid to the developing countries of Asia?

A. Association of South East Asia Nations
B. International Development Association
C. Asian Development Bank
D. None of the above

Q.18 Suspicious Transactions Reports (STRs) is submitted to _________.

A. RBI
B. Banking Department, Ministry of Finance
C. FIU-IND
D. Central Bureau of Investigation (CBI)

Q.19 Which section of Banking Regulation Act 1949 provides nomination for payment of depositor's money?

A. Section 42
B. Section 24

C. Section 110A

D. Section 45ZA

Q.20 Planning is which kind of process?

A. Goal Oriented

B. Flexible

C. Time bound

D. All of these

Q.21 Which of the following financial reports shows the profitability of a business?

A. Income statement

B. Balance sheet

C. Cash flow statement

D. Statement of changes in equity

Q.22 For the purpose of an inquiry under the MRTP Act, the commission has the power equivalent to

A. Civil court

B. Consumer court

C. High court

D. None of these

Q.23 _________ is the reason for bank passbook showing a higher balance than Cashbook.

A. Cheque issued but not paid

B. Interest charged by Bank

C. Direct payment made by Bank

D. Cheque deposited but not cleared

Q.24 Laissez -faire policy is adopted in

A. Socialist Economic system

B. Capitalist Economic system

C. Mixed Economic System

D. Communist Economic System

Q.25 Which of the following skills is equally important at all levels of management?

A. Technical skill

B. Human relation skill

C. Conceptual skill

D. All of the above

Q.26 Assets minus liabilities equal to _________.

A. Goodwill

B. Working capital

C. Net income

D. Capital

Q.27 Which of the following financial statements shows the movement of cash and cash equivalents during an accounting period?

A. Income statement

B. Balance sheet

C. Cash flow statement

D. Statement of changes in equity

Q.28 Which one of the following formulae are used to calculate "Cross Relationship" under the span of control?

A. $n (n - 1)$

B. $n (\frac{2n}{2} - 1)$

C. $n (\frac{2n}{2} + n -1)$

D. None of the above

Q.29 Which of the following is not an advantage of MBO?

A. Success without planning

B. Employee commitment

C. Better appraisal

D. Self control

Q.30 Motivational process and not the motivators as such is associated with the _________.

A. Need hierarchy theory

B. Two-factor theory

C. ERG Theory

D. Expectancy theory

Q.31 Which one of the following is the oldest form of organization?

A. Functional organization

B. Staff organization

C. Line organization

D. Departmentation

Q.32 Goodwill is classified as which one of the following assets?

A. Fixed

B. Long term

C. Current

D. Intangible

Q.33 Correlation between price and demand is _________.

A. Negative

B. Positive

C. Zero

D. None of these

Q.34 Insurance & Freight on machinery purchased is _________.

A. Capital expenditure

B. Prepaid expenses

C. Revenue expenditure

D. Deferred revenue expenditure

Q.35 The collection of integrated and related master files is known as _________.

A. Database

B. Table

C. Record

D. Field

Q.36 In the field of management some of the important techniques, relate to budgeting, cost accounting, planning and control are through _________.

A. Operational research

B. PERT and CPM

C. Budgetary control

D. Financial administration

Q.37 Current assets are also known as _____.

A. Gross working capital

B. Invested capital

C. Assets

D. Cash

Q.38 A series of actions or operations that convert inputs into outputs is known as _________.

A. Information

B. Data

C. Processing

D. Facts

Q.39 Noting charges are paid in the event of _______ of a bill.

A. Withdrawal

B. Dishonour

C. Deposit

D. Payment

Q.40 Depreciation is incorporated in cash flows because it _______.

A. Is unavoidable cost

B. Is a cash flow
C. Involves an outflow
D. Reduces tax liability

Q.41 Which one is more appropriate for the cost of retained earnings?
A. Weighted Average cost of capital
B. Opportunity cost to the firm
C. Expected rate of return by the investor
D. None of the above

Q.42 Debt financing is a cheaper source of finance because of ______.
A. Time value of money
B. Rate of interest
C. Tax-deductibility of interest
D. Dividends are not payable to lenders

Q.43 The statement of Banking definition is given by ______.
A. T.G. Hart
B. White Head
C. Kinely
D. All of these

Q.44 The expenses related to the main operations of a business are referred to as ______.
A. Administration expense
B. Non-administration expense
C. Selling expense
D. Operating expense

Q.45 A current asset that is convertible to cash within 3 months can be referred to as ______.
A. Cash asset
B. Operating asset
C. Intangible assets
D. Cash equivalent

Q.46 The conflicts in project ranking in capital budgeting as per NPV and IRR may arise because of:
A. Size disparity
B. Time disparity
C. Life disparity
D. All of the above

Q.47 Capital gearing ratio indicates the relationship between:
A. Assets and capital
B. Loans and capital
C. Equity shareholders fund and long term borrowed funds
D. Debentures and share capital

Q.48 ZBB stands for
A. Zero Base Budgeting
B. Zero Basel Budgeting
C. Zero Bond Budget
D. None of the above

Q.49 The stock turnover ratio is ___.
A. Financial ratio
B. Activity ratio
C. Solvency ratio
D. Profitability ratio

Q.50 AS-19 deals with ______.
A. Borrowing costs
B. Earning per share
C. Leases
D. Segment reporting

Q.51 What is depreciation?

A. Cost of a fixed asset
B. Cost of a fixed asset's repair
C. The residual value of a fixed asset
D. A portion of a fixed asset's cost consumed during the current accounting period

Q.52 The stock turnover ratio may be calculated as ______.
A. Cost of goods sold/Average stock
B. Turnover at cost/stock at cost
C. Turnover at selling price/Stock at a selling price
D. All of the above

Q.53 ROI stands for ____.
A. Return on Investment
B. Ratio of Investment
C. Return of Income
D. None of these

Q.54 The satisfactory ratio between internal and external equity is ___.
A. 1:1
B. 2:1
C. 3:1
D. 4:1

Q.55 Under which depreciation method, the amount of depreciation expenses remains the same throughout the life of the asset?
A. Straight-line method
B. Reducing balance method
C. Number of units produced a method
D. Machine hours method

Q.56 Which is wage determination factors?
A. Prevailing Rates of Wages
B. Cost of Living
C. Ability to Pay
D. All of the above

Q.57 A company purchased a vehicle for Rs. $6,000$. It will be used for 5 years and its residual value is expected to be Rs. $1,000$. What is the annual amount of depreciation using the straight-line method of depreciation?
A. Rs. $1,000$
B. Rs. $2,000$
C. Rs. $3,000$
D. Rs. $5,000$

Q.58 Which of the following techniques of performance appraisal is least susceptible to personal bias?
A. BARS
B. Rating scale
C. Checklist
D. Critical incident

Q.59 Which of the following is the normal balance of an accumulated depreciation account?
A. Debit balance
B. Credit balance
C. Nil balance
D. All the above

Q.60 How the trial balance shows the accumulated depreciation?
A. As a debit item
B. As a credit item
C. It doesn't show
D. None of these

Q.61 An alternative term used for accumulated depreciation expenses ______.

A. Provision for depreciation
B. Cumulative depreciation
C. Targeted depreciation
D. Depletion

Q.62 Tax receipts are examples of _________ expense in nature.
A. Revenue   B. Capital
C. Financial   D. Extraordinary

Q.63 Balance of Payment can be made favorable if _______.
A. Exports are increased
B. Imports are increased
C. Devaluation of money
D. Both (A) and (C)

Q.64 Which facility was established to provide assistance to members facing payments difficulties that are large in relation to their economies and their fund quotas?
A. Supplementary Financing Facility (SFF)
B. Compensatory and Contingency Financing Facility (CCFF)
C. Extended Fund Facility (EFF)
D. Bufferstock Financing Facility (BFF)

Q.65 Quotas of all IMF members are reviewed at intervals of _________.

A. Five years
B. Not more than five years
C. Three years
D. Two years

Q.66 What are the characteristics of the loans provided by the International Development Association (IDA) to member countries?
A. They are on liberal terms with regard to the rate of interest
B. They are on liberal terms with regard to the period of repayment
C. They can be repaid in the currency of the member country
D. All of the above

Q.67 Which of the following is the best example of an agreement between Oligopolists?
A. GATT   B. OPEC   C. WTO   D. UNIDO

Q.68 Which type of subsidies are provided to industrial research and pro-competitive development activity in disadvantaged regions?
A. Prohibited subsidies
B. Actionable subsidies
C. Non-actionable subsidies
D. None of the above

Q.69 A cash book that is used to record the small payments of cash is generally referred to as
A. Simple cash book
B. Two columns of the cash book
C. Three columns of the cash book
D. Petty cash book

Q.70 Debt equity ratio calculated as part of ratio analysis, indicates
A. Repayment capacity of loans
B. Profitability performance of the firm
C. Strength of the firm to attract long term borrowed funds
D. The liquidity position of the firm

Q.71 Which of the following point is responsibility for effective market segmentation?
A. Measurability   B. Easy & accessibility
C. Substantiality   D. All of the above

Q.72 Marketing Process involves _______.
A. Product   B. Demand Flow
C. Human Needs   D. All of these

Q.73 A limited company is a/an _________ person.
A. Original   B. Artificial
C. Duplicate   D. None of the above

Q.74 Which research includes all types of researchers into human motives when it refers to qualitative research designed to uncover the consumer's subconsciousness or hidden motivations?
A. Motivational Research
B. Marketing Research
C. Managerial Research
D. Price Research

Q.75 What is the "Fundamental Premise of Economics"?
A. Individuals are capable of establishing goals and acting in a manner consistent with achievement of those goals
B. Natural resources will always be scare
C. Individuals choose the alternative for which they believe the net gains to be the greatest
D. No matter what the circumstances, individual choice always involve a tradeoff

Q.76 The human relations approach of management is associated with
A. Abraham Maslow   B. Peter F. Drucker
C. Elton Mayo   D. Herzberg

Q.77 In perfect competition, in the long run, there will be no _______.
A. Normal profits   B. Supernormal profits
C. Production   D. Costs

Q.78 Which of the following is a non-current liability?
A. Bills payable   B. Sundry creditors
C. Bank overdraft   D. Long term loans

Q.79 Kyoto Protocol is relating to _________.
A. Competition
B. Consumer protection
C. Environment protection
D. Atomic energy generation

Q.80 Bank classifications according to the law are
A. Private bank

B. Scheduled bank

C. Non-scheduled bank

D. Both (B) and (C)

Q.81 Purchase of office equipment for cash will be recorded on which side of a cash book?

A. Receipts

B. Payments

C. Incomes

D. Expenditures

Q.82 Postdated cheques are considered as:

A. Cash

B. Bank balance

C. Accounts receivable

D. Cash reserve

Q.83 Postage stamps on hand are considered as_________.

A. Bank balance

B. Prepaid expenses

C. Accounts receivable

D. Creditors

Q.84 Petty cash fund is supposed to be replenished:

A. Every year

B. Every half-year

C. Every year

D. At the end of every accounting period

Q.85 A credit balance in the cash book indicates:

A. Bank balance

B. Cash at the bank

C. Bank overdraft

D. The bank under draft

Q.86 Consistency with reference to application of accounting principles refer to the:

A. All the companies in the same industries should use identical procedures and methods

B. Income and assets have not been overstated

C. Accounting methods and procedures used have to be consistently applied from year to year

D. Any accounting method or procedure can be utilized

Q.87 Which of the following of the journal or ledger given under is not correct?

A. Journal is a book of original entry

B. Journal is a book of analytical record

C. Ledger is a book of secondary record

D. The process of The recording of transaction in the ledger is called posting

Q.88 Unpresented cheques are also referred to as:

A. Uncollected cheques

B. Uncredited cheques

C. Outstanding cheques

D. Bounced cheques

Q.89 Accrued expenses are considered as_______.

A. Asset   **B.** Liability   **C.** Gain   **D.** Income

Q.90 Prepaid expenses are considered as______.

A. Asset   **B.** Liability   **C.** Loss   **D.** Capital

Q.91 Earned but not yet received income is treated as_______.

A. Liability   **B.** Asset   **C.** Loss   **D.** Capital

Q.92 Revenue earned but not yet received by the business is known as:

A. Contra asset revenue

B. Accrued expenses

C. Accrued revenue

D. Unearned revenue

Q.93 Using 'lower of cost and net realizable value' for the purpose of inventory valuation is the implementation of which of the following concepts?

A. The going concern concept

B. The separate entity concept

C. The prudence concept

D. Matching concept

Q.94 The concept of 'separate entity' is applicable to which of the following types of businesses?

A. Sole proprietorship

B. Corporation

C. Partnership

D. All of the above

Q.95 Does the prudence concept allow a business to build substantially higher reserves or provisions than that are actually required?

A. Yes

B. No

C. To some extent

D. It depends on the type of business.

Q.96 The revenue recognition principle dictates that all types of incomes should be recorded or recognized:

A. Cash is received.

B. At the end of the accounting period

C. When they are earned.

D. When interest is paid.

Q.97 The matching concept matches which of the following?

A. Asset with liabilities

B. Capital with income

C. Revenues with expenses

D. Expenses with capital

Q.98 The allocation of the owner's private expenses to his/her business violates which of the following?

A. Accrual concept

B. Matching concept

C. Separate business entity concept

D. Consistency concept

Q.99 Which of the following is the time span into which the total life of a business is divided for the purpose of preparing financial statements?

A. Fiscal year

B. Calendar year

C. Accounting period

D. Accrual period

Q.100 General Journal is a book of _____ entries.

A. First

B. Original

C. Secondary

D. Generic

Q.101 Mr. X sold goods to Mr. Y ask Mr. X to keep the goods with him for some time:

A. Symbolic delivery
B. Actual delivery
C. Constructive delivery
D. None of these

Q.102 If nothing is written about the accounting assumption to be followed it is presumed that:
A. They have been followed.
B. They have not been followed.
C. They are followed to some extent.
D. None of these

Q.103 Capital account is a ______ account.
A. Personal
B. Real
C. Nominal
D. None of the above

Q.104 Cash account is a ______ account.
A. Personal
B. Real
C. Nominal
D. None of the above

Q.105 The principle "Debit the receiver and credit the giver" is related to______.
A. Personal account
B. Real account
C. Nominal account
D. None of the above

Q.106 If the original and current price of a machinery is given, it will be recorded at which value?
A. Historical value
B. Realisable value
C. Market value
D. Original cost

Q.107 Sales – Gross Profit = ______
A. Cost of goods sold
B. Net sales
C. Gross Sales
D. Liabilities

Q.108 Which of the following is a real account?
A. Building account
B. Capital account
C. Discount received account
D. Rent account

Q.109 Valuation of stock in accounting follows the principle of cost price or ____ whichever is lower.
A. Market Price
B. Average Price
C. Net realizable Value
D. None of these

Q.110 Which of the following is not a nominal Account?
A. Outstanding salaries Account
B. Salaries account
C. Interest paid
D. Commission received

Q.111 Mr. X is a dealer in electronic goods (refrigerator, washing machine, air conditioners, televisions, etc.) He purchased two air conditioners and installed them in his showroom. In the books of X, the cost of two air conditioners will be debited to:
A. Drawing account
B. Capital account
C. Fixed assets
D. Purchases account

Q.112 A trader calculated his profit as Rs.150000 on 31/03/2014. It is an:

A. Transaction
B. Event
C. Transaction as well as the event
D. Neither transaction nor event

Q.113 For every debit, there will be an equal credit according to:
A. Matching concept
B. Cost concept
C. Money measurement concept
D. Dual aspect concept

Q.114 Historical cost concept requires the valuation of an asset at:
A. Original cost
B. Replacement value
C. Net realizable value
D. Market value

Q.115 The comparison of the financial statement of one year with that of another is possible only when the______________concept is followed.
A. Going concerned
B. Accrual
C. Consistency
D. Materiality

Q.116 Profit and loss is calculated at the stage of:
A. Recording
B. Posting
C. Classifying
D. Summarising

Q.117 Which of the following is not the main objective of accounting?
A. Systematic recording of transactions
B. Ascertaining profit or los
C. Ascertainment of financial position
D. Solving tax disputes with tax authorities

Q.118 A company incorporated outside India but has a place of business in India is termed as__________.
A. Statutory company
B. Holding company
C. Subsidiary company
D. Foreign company

Q.119 The rule debit all expenses and losses and credit all income and gains relates to:
A. Personal account
B. Real account
C. Nominal account
D. All of the above

Q.120 The matching concept means:
A. Assets = Capital + Liabilities
B. Transactions recorded at accrual concept
C. Anticipate no profit but recognize all losses
D. Expenses should be matched with the revenue of the period

// Smart Answer Sheet //

Correct Indicates percentage of students who answered questions correctly.

Skipped Indicates percentage of students who skipped questions.

Q.	Ans.	Correct / Skipped
1	C	58.46 % / 16.54 %
2	C	27.69 % / 33.08 %
3	D	24.23 % / 27.69 %
4	C	10.77 % / 34.23 %
5	B	55.0 % / 31.92 %
6	A	20.0 % / 31.92 %
7	B	24.62 % / 33.84 %
8	C	32.69 % / 33.85 %
9	C	31.54 % / 34.23 %
10	A	50.0 % / 33.46 %
11	B	34.62 % / 30.0 %
12	B	37.69 % / 34.23 %
13	B	53.85 % / 25.77 %
14	B	21.92 % / 34.23 %
15	C	33.46 % / 28.08 %
16	B	33.46 % / 29.23 %
17	C	46.15 % / 33.85 %
18	C	45.0 % / 34.23 %
19	D	58.85 % / 9.23 %
20	D	53.85 % / 26.53 %
21	A	26.54 % / 23.46 %
22	A	26.54 % / 34.23 %
23	A	45.38 % / 16.16 %
24	B	26.15 % / 34.23 %
25	B	10.38 % / 33.47 %
26	D	37.31 % / 34.23 %
27	C	58.08 % / 21.54 %
28	C	24.62 % / 34.61 %
29	A	38.85 % / 24.61 %
30	D	12.31 % / 32.31 %
31	C	24.62 % / 30.0 %
32	D	56.92 % / 28.08 %
33	A	33.46 % / 18.85 %
34	A	33.08 % / 34.23 %
35	A	50.0 % / 28.46 %
36	B	26.54 % / 30.0 %
37	A	30.38 % / 33.47 %
38	C	43.46 % / 33.46 %
39	B	42.69 % / 34.23 %
40	D	24.23 % / 34.23 %
41	B	15.38 % / 23.85 %
42	C	16.15 % / 34.23 %
43	D	32.31 % / 28.84 %
44	D	42.69 % / 34.23 %
45	D	39.23 % / 25.39 %
46	D	44.62 % / 34.23 %
47	C	35.77 % / 30.77 %
48	A	43.46 % / 34.23 %
49	B	23.85 % / 34.23 %
50	C	31.15 % / 33.85 %
51	D	46.92 % / 27.7 %
52	A	37.31 % / 26.92 %
53	A	52.31 % / 33.46 %
54	A	31.15 % / 32.31 %
55	A	54.23 % / 30.39 %
56	D	46.54 % / 33.84 %
57	A	47.31 % / 33.46 %
58	A	26.92 % / 33.46 %
59	B	18.85 % / 30.0 %
60	B	22.31 % / 27.31 %
61	A	26.15 % / 33.47 %
62	A	41.92 % / 33.46 %
63	D	41.54 % / 29.61 %
64	A	18.08 % / 33.07 %
65	B	21.15 % / 32.7 %
66	D	46.92 % / 32.7 %
67	B	23.85 % / 33.46 %
68	C	19.62 % / 33.84 %
69	D	48.46 % / 33.46 %
70	C	28.85 % / 34.23 %
71	D	69.62 % / 18.84 %
72	D	60.77 % / 28.08 %
73	B	48.08 % / 34.23 %
74	A	31.92 % / 33.46 %
75	C	15.77 % / 33.08 %
76	C	31.15 % / 31.93 %
77	B	38.46 % / 33.46 %
78	D	39.23 % / 33.46 %
79	C	39.62 % / 20.38 %
80	D	61.92 % / 28.46 %

Q.	Ans.	Correct / Skipped
81	B	36.54 % / 24.23 %
82	C	47.69 % / 33.08 %
83	B	42.31 % / 33.84 %
84	D	51.92 % / 31.54 %
85	C	38.85 % / 33.46 %
86	C	30.77 % / 33.85 %
87	B	36.92 % / 34.23 %
88	C	33.08 % / 34.23 %

Q.	Ans.	Correct / Skipped
89	B	40.0 % / 33.85 %
90	A	41.92 % / 34.23 %
91	B	40.77 % / 33.85 %
92	C	38.08 % / 34.23 %
93	C	39.62 % / 25.0 %
94	D	43.08 % / 34.23 %
95	B	19.23 % / 31.15 %
96	C	33.85 % / 31.92 %

Q.	Ans.	Correct / Skipped
97	C	30.0 % / 33.85 %
98	C	46.15 % / 33.85 %
99	C	41.15 % / 31.54 %
100	B	48.08 % / 29.61 %
101	A	29.62 % / 33.07 %
102	B	15.38 % / 34.24 %
103	A	26.92 % / 33.46 %
104	B	46.92 % / 31.54 %

Q.	Ans.	Correct / Skipped
105	A	46.15 % / 33.08 %
106	D	27.31 % / 34.23 %
107	A	43.46 % / 28.46 %
108	A	29.23 % / 34.23 %
109	C	29.23 % / 25.0 %
110	A	36.92 % / 33.85 %
111	C	26.54 % / 20.38 %
112	B	22.69 % / 33.85 %

Q.	Ans.	Correct / Skipped
113	D	53.85 % / 21.92 %
114	A	33.08 % / 34.23 %
115	C	28.85 % / 31.15 %
116	D	42.31 % / 34.23 %
117	D	61.15 % / 21.16 %
118	D	44.62 % / 33.84 %
119	C	56.54 % / 21.54 %
120	D	37.69 % / 27.69 %

Performance Analysis	
Avg. Score (%)	33.0%
Toppers Score (%)	99.0%
Your Score	

//Hints and Solutions//

1. The demand curve is a graphical representation of the relationship between the price of a good or service and the quantity demanded for a given period of time. In a typical representation, the price will appear on the left vertical axis, the quantity demanded on the horizontal axis.

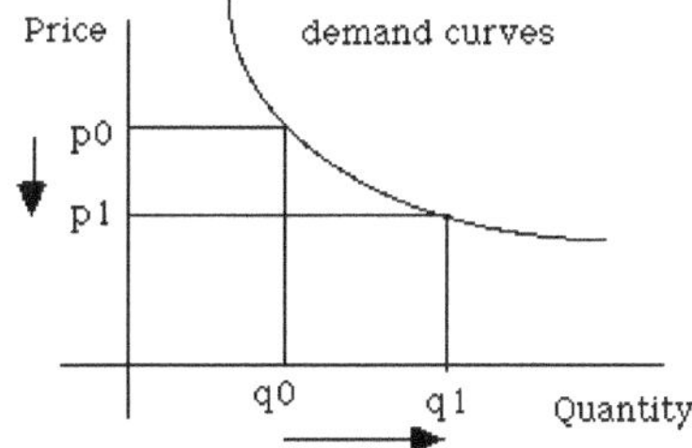

Hence, the correct option is (C).

2. A bilateral monopoly exists when a market has only one supplier and one buyer. The one supplier will tend to act as monopoly power and look to charge high prices to the one buyer. The lone buyer will look towards paying a price that is as low as possible.

Hence, the correct option is (C).

3. Land on lease should be shown in the balance sheet contrary to the fact that the company does not own that piece of land is the implementation of Substance over form concept. Substance over form is the concept that the financial statements and accompanying disclosures of a business should reflect the underlying realities of accounting transactions.

Hence, the correct option is (D).

4. Task structure refers to the degree to which the task is made clear to the employee who has to perform it. Task structure includes the extent to which tasks are defined and have detailed job descriptions and procedures.

Hence, the correct option is (C).

5. A duopoly is a situation where 2 companies together own all, or nearly all, of the market for a given product or service. A duopoly is the most basic form of oligopoly, a market dominated by a small number of companies.

Hence, the correct option is (B).

6. Depreciation is charged on fixed assets to comply with the matching concept which requires that revenues must be matched with associated expenses to get a complete and accurate picture of profit and loss. The matching principle states that the related revenues and expenses must be matched in the same period. This is done in order to link the costs of an asset or revenue to its benefits.

Hence, the correct option is (A).

7. Net profit is computed in the income statement. Net income, also called net profit, is a calculation that measures the number of total revenues that exceed total expenses. In other words, it shows how much revenues are left over after all expenses have been paid.

Hence, the correct option is (B).

8. In case of Education cess, the assessee had claimed deduction of the Education and Higher Secondary cess, levied on the Income Tax payable by the assessee, from its taxable income of the Profit and Gains of Business or Profession on the ground that "Cess" is neither Tax nor Rate, hence is not disallowable u/s 40. The Assessing Officer did not allow the deduction of such cess while determining the taxable income of Profit and Gains of Business or Profession.

Hence, the correct option is (C).

9. As per section 40(B), only that salary, remuneration, bonus, commission, etc payable to working partners or any payment of interest payable to any partner will be allowed as deduction only if it is authorized by the partnership deed.

Hence, the correct option is (C).

10. Balance sheet financial statements show the financial position of a business at a specific date. The balance sheet, sometimes called the statement of financial position, lists the company's assets, liabilities, and stockholders ' equity (including dollar amounts) as of a specific moment in time. That specific moment is the close of business on the date of the balance sheet.

Hence, the correct option is (A).

11. A loss from business or profession can be set off against all income heads other than salary while losses from a speculative activity or owning/maintaining racehorses can be adjusted only against profits under the respective heads.

Hence, the correct option is (B).

12. Guarantee for the employer for the loss out of employees dishonest is fidelity insurance. A Fidelity Insurance policy covers losses sustained by the employer as a result of an act of forgery, fraud or dishonesty from an employee.

Hence, the correct option is (B).

13. RBI report on currency and finance. According to the Reserve Bank of India's annual report on currency and finance for 2005-06, released on 31 May, "it is imperative that the financial markets are developed further," if the risks of financial integration are to be mitigated.

Hence, the correct option is (B).

14. SEZs were introduced to India in 2000, following the already successful SEZ model used in China. India relied on export processing zones (EPZs) which failed to make an impact on foreign investors. By 2005, all EPZs had been converted to SEZs.

Hence, the correct option is (B).

15. In order to control credit, the Reserve Bank of India should Increase CRR and increase the Bank rate. During high inflation in the economy, RBI raises the CRR to lower the bank's loanable funds.

Hence, the correct option is (C).

16. Presently there are 43 RRBs in India Since 1 April 2020. Currently, there are 43 RRBs in India and each RRB is sponsored by the Government of India along with the State Government and Sponsor bank.

Hence, the correct option is (B).

17. The Asian Development Bank provides assistance to its developing member countries, the private sector, and public-private partnerships through grants, loans, technical assistance, and equity investments to promote development. The Asian Development Bank regularly facilitates policy dialogues and provides advisory services.

Hence, the correct option is (C).

18. The Government of India set up the Financial Intelligence Unit – India (FIU-IND) on 18th November 2004 as an independent body to report directly to the Economic Intelligence Council (EIC) headed by the Finance Minister.

If a reporting entity suspects or has reasonable grounds to suspect that funds are the proceeds of criminal activity, or are related to terrorist financing, it shall as soon as possible but no later than 3 days report promptly its suspicions to the Financial Intelligence Unit (FIU).

Hence, the correct option is (C).

19. Sections 45ZA to 45ZF of the Banking Regulation Act, 1949 provide, inter alia, for the following matters to enable a co-operative bank to make payment to the nominee of a deceased depositor, of the amount standing to the credit of the depositor.

Hence, the correct option is (D).

20. Planning is the process of thinking about the activities required to achieve the desired goal. It is the first and foremost activity to achieve the desired results. It involves the creation and maintenance of a plan, such as psychological aspects that require conceptual skills.

Hence, the correct option is (D).

21. The income statement shows the profitability of a business. The income statement is the most important report for many analysts. It shows the company's operating results for an entire year.

Hence, the correct option is (A).

22. The Commission shall, for the purpose of any inquiry under the Act, have the same powers as are vested in a civil court under the Civil Procedure Code while trying a suit, in respect of certain matters.

Hence, the correct option is (A).

23. When a business compares the balance of its cash book with the balance shown by the bank passbook, there is often a difference, which is caused by the time gap in recording the transactions relating either to payments or receipts. Cheque issued by the bank but not yet presented for payment is one reason for bank passbook showing higher balance than cash book. When cheques are issued by the firm to suppliers or creditors of the firm, these are immediately entered on the credit side of the cash book. However, the receiving party may not present the cheque o the bank for payment immediately. The bank will debit the firm's account only when these cheques are actually paid by the bank. Hence, there is a time lag between the issue of a cheque and its presentation to the bank which may cause the difference between the two balances.

Hence, the correct option is (A).

24. Laissez-faire is an economic philosophy of free-market capitalism. The theory of Laissez-faire was developed by the French Physiocrats during the 18th century. Capitalism is often thought of as an economic system in which private actors own and control property in accord with their interests, and demand and supply freely set prices in markets in a way that can serve the best interests of society. The essential feature of capitalism is the motive to make a profit.

Hence, the correct option is (B).

25. Technical skills are most important for lower-level managers, human skills are equally important at all levels of management, and conceptual skills and motivation to manage an increase in importance as managers rise through the managerial ranks.

Hence, the correct option is (B).

26. Assets minus liabilities equal to capital, it shows that a company's total amount of assets equals the total amount of liabilities plus owner's (or stockholders') equity.

Hence, the correct option is (D).

27. The cash flow statement shows the movement of cash and cash equivalents during an accounting period. A cash flow statement, also known as the statement of cash flows or funds flow statement, is a financial statement that shows how changes in balance sheet accounts and income affect cash and cash equivalents, and breaks the analysis down to operating, investing, and financing activities.

Hence, the correct option is (C).

28. On the basis of the analysis of relationships, Giraincunas developed the following mathematical formula based on the geometric increase in the complexities of managing;

$$N\left[\left(\frac{2n}{2}\right) + (n-1)\right]$$

Where n indicates the number of subordinates supervised.

Hence, the correct option is (C).

29.

- The "Management by Objective" (MBO) is a model of strategic management that aims at improving an organization's performance by identifying clearly defined objectives for both management & staff.

- According to the theory, engagement, and commitment/dedication amongst workers and the alignment of goals within the company is promoted by having a say in goal setting and action plans. The strategy was formulated by "Peter Drucker" in the 1950s.

- The benefits include workers who take pride in their jobs and accomplish goals and comprise advantages such as better planning & organization, self-control, better appraisal of performance, & executive development. This also blends workers with their talents, expertise, and learning opportunities.

- Moreover, MBO contributes to better communication between management and employees. The assigning of tailored goals gives staff a sense of commitment and loyalty to the organization. Eventually, the management will accomplish goals that can contribute to the company's success.

Hence, the correct option is (A).

30. Expectancy theory (or expectancy theory of motivation) proposes that an individual will behave or act in a certain way because they are motivated to select a specific behaviour over others due to what they expect the result of that selected behaviour will be. In essence, the motivation of the behaviour selection is determined by the desirability of the outcome. However, at the core of the theory is the cognitive process of how an individual processes the different motivational elements. This is done before making the ultimate choice. The outcome is not the sole determining factor in making the decision of how to behave.

Hence, the correct option is (D).

31. Line organization is the simplest and the oldest type of organization. It is also known as a scalar organization or military type of organization. In the words of J.M. Lundy, "It is characterized by direct lines of authority flowing from the top to the bottom of the organizational hierarchy and lines of responsibility flowing in an opposite but equally direct manner."

Hence, the correct option is (C).

32. Goodwill is classified as Intangible assets. The goodwill amounts to the excess of the "purchase consideration" (the money paid to purchase the asset or business) over the total value of the assets and liabilities. It is classified as an intangible asset on the balance sheet since it can neither be seen nor touched.

Hence, the correct option is (D).

33. The law of demand is an economic principle that explains the negative correlation between the price of a good or service and its demand. If all other factors remain the same when the price of a good or service increases, the demand decreases, and vice versa.

Hence, the correct option is (A).

34. Insurance & Freight on machinery purchased is Capital Expenditure. Capital expenditure refers to funds that are used by a company to acquire, improve, or maintain long term assets to improve the efficiency of earning capacity of the company. Capital Expenditures are for fixed assets, which are expected to be productive assets for a long period of time. All the amount paid up to the point an asset is ready for use is included in the cost of that asset. So, Insurance and freight on machinery purchased are included in the cost of machinery.

Hence, the correct option is (A).

35. A database is an integrated collection of logically related records or files. The data is managed by systems software called database management systems (DBMS).

Hence, the correct option is (A).

36. PERT and CPM are techniques of project management useful in the basic managerial functions of planning, scheduling, and control. PERT stands for "Programme Evaluation & Review Technique" and CPM is the abbreviation for "Critical Path Method". These days the projects undertaken by business houses are very large and take a number of years before commercial production can start.

Hence, the correct option is (B).

37. Current assets are also known as gross working capital. Gross working capital is the sum of all of a company's current assets (assets that are convertible to cash within a year or less).

Hence, the correct option is (A).

38. A series of actions or operations that convert inputs into outputs is known as processing. Operations management transforms inputs (labour, capital, equipment, land, buildings, materials, and information) into outputs (goods and services) that provide added value to customers.

Hence, the correct option is (C).

39. Noting charges are paid in the event of dishonour of a bill. Noting is the recording of the fact of dishonour by a notary public which becomes evidence of dishonour. When a bill of exchange is dishonour, in order to prove the fact, the holder may get the bill noted. Charges paid on noting are called as noting charges.

Hence, the correct option is (B).

40. The use of depreciation can reduce taxes that can ultimately help to increase net income. Net income is then used as a starting point in calculating a company's operating cash flow. Operating cash flow starts with net income, then adds depreciation/amortization, the net change in operating working capital, and other operating cash flow adjustments. The result is a higher amount of cash on the cash flow statement because depreciation is added back into the operating cash flow.

Ultimately, depreciation does not negatively affect the operating cash flow of the business.

Hence, the correct option is (D).

41. The opportunity cost to the firm is more appropriate for the cost of retained earnings. The opportunity cost of the firm includes explicit cost as well as implicit cost.

Hence, the correct option is (B).

42. Debt financing is considered a cheaper source of financing not only because it is less expensive in terms of interest, but also and issuance costs than any other form of security but due to availability of tax benefits; the interest payment on a debt is deductible as a tax expense.

Hence, the correct option is (C).

43. A bank statement is a document that is issued by a bank once a month to its customers, listing the transactions impacting a bank account. The statement provides the following information:

The beginning cash balance in the account.

The total amount of each deposited batch of checks and cash.

Funds are withdrawn from the account.

Individual checks paid.

Interest earned on the account.

Service fees and penalties charged against the account.

Ending cash balance in the account.

Hence, the correct option is (D).

44. The expenses related to the main operations of a business are referred to as operating expenses. The operating expenses refer to the specific costs after gross revenue is defined in the income statement.

Hence, the correct option is (D).

45. A current asset that is convertible to cash within 3 months can be referred to as cash equivalent. Cash and cash equivalents refer to the line item on the balance sheet that reports the value of a company's assets that are cash or can be converted into cash immediately.

Hence, the correct option is (D).

46. The conflict either arises due to the relative size of the project or due to the different cash flow distribution of the projects. Since NPV is an absolute measure, it will rank a project adding more dollar value higher regardless of the initial investment required.

Hence, the correct option is (D).

47. Capital gearing is a British term that refers to the amount of debt a company has relative to its equity. In the United States, capital gearing is known as "financial leverage". Companies with high capital gearing will have a large amount of debt relative to their equity. The gearing ratio is a measure of financial risk and expresses the amount of a company's debt in terms of its equity. A company with a gearing ratio of 2.0 would have twice as much debt as equity.

Hence, the correct option is (C).

48. Zero Base Budgeting (ZBB) is a method of budgeting in which all expenses must be justified for each new period. The process of zero-based budgeting starts from a "zero base," and every function within an organization is analyzed for its needs and costs.

Hence, the correct option is (A).

49. The Stock turnover ratio is the most important activity ratio as it helps in understanding the relationship between inventory/average stock and the cost of goods sold. The Stock turnover ratio is also known as the inventory turnover ratio or stock velocity ratio as it indicates the speed of stock conversion into sales or revenue.

Hence, the correct option is (B).

50. A lease is a transaction whereby an agreement is entered into by the lessor with the lessee for the right to use an asset by the lessee in return for a payment or series of payments for an agreed period of time.

Hence, the correct option is (C).

51. The portion of a fixed asset's cost consumed during the current accounting period is known as depreciation. Depreciation is an accounting method of allocating the cost of a tangible asset over its useful life and is used to account for declines in value. Businesses depreciate long-term assets for both tax and accounting purposes.

Hence, the correct option is (D).

52. Inventory turnover indicates how many times a company sells and replaces its stock of goods during a particular period. The formula for inventory turnover ratio is the cost of goods sold divided by the average inventory for the same period.

Hence, the correct option is (A).

53. Return on Investment (ROI) is a performance measure used to evaluate the efficiency of an investment or compare the efficiency of a number of different investments. ROI tries to directly measure the amount of return on a particular investment, relative to the investment's cost.

Hence, the correct option is (A).

54. The satisfactory ratio between internal and external equity is 1:1.

Internal equity is how one employee's pay package compares to others inside the same organization. External equity compares a pay package to others outside the organization. In this case, the word "equity" refers to "fairness" or "equivalence" and has nothing to do with share-based (equity-based) compensation.

Hence, the correct option is (A).

55. Under the straight-line method, the amount of depreciation expenses remains the same throughout the life of the asset. In a straight-line depreciation method, it is assumed that the asset uniformly depreciates over its useful life.

Hence, the correct option is (A).

56. Demand and supply are one of the important factors which influence the wage rates. If the number of workers required is more than the availability of workers, then employees will be paid a higher rate of work and vice versa.

Hence, the correct option is (D).

57. Cost of the asset = Rs. $6,000$

Salvage Value = Rs. $1,000$

Total Depreciation Cost = Cost of asset – Salvage Value $=$ $6,000 - 1,000 = Rs.\ 5,000$

The useful life of the asset = 5 years

Thus, annual depreciation cost = (Cost of asset − Salvage Cost)/Useful Life $= \dfrac{5,000}{5}$ = Rs. **1,000**.

Hence, the correct option is (A).

58. BARS is least susceptible to personal bias. BARS is also known as the behavioral expectation scale. BARS stands for Behaviourally Anchored Rating Scale. It is a method to rate the performance of the employees. BARS are normally presented vertically with scale points ranging from five to nine.

Hence, the correct option is (A).

59. A credit balance is the normal balance of an accumulated depreciation account. Accumulated depreciation has a credit balance because it aggregates the amount of depreciation expense charged against a fixed asset.

Hence, the correct option is (B).

60. The trial balance shows the accumulated depreciation as a credit item. Accumulated depreciation has a credit balance because it aggregates the amount of depreciation expense charged against a fixed asset.

Hence, the correct option is (B).

61. Provision for depreciation is an alternative term used for accumulated depreciation expenses. Depreciation expense is recognized on the income statement as a non-cash expense that reduces the company's net income.

Hence, the correct option is (A).

62. Tax receipts are an example of revenue expenses. These are recurring expenses for an organization, hence fall under revenue expenditure. These receipts are a major source of income for any kind of business and without them, a business can't survive for long. This is a result of normal and core business activities. Being a normal business result is the reason for its recurring nature.

Hence, the correct option is (A).

63. Balance of payments or balance of the account is a more comprehensive term. The balance of trade will be favorable if the value of exports exceeds the value of imports or unfavorable if the value of imports exceeds the value of exports. In both cases, the difference of only visible items is taken into account.

Hence, the correct option is (D).

64. Balance of payments difficulties can arise and, in the worst case, build into crises even in the face of strong prevention efforts. The IMF assists countries in restoring economic stability by helping to devise programs of corrective policies and providing loans to support them. The SFF allowed countries with Stand by or Extended Arrangements to obtain supplementary and parallel credits financed by the borrowed resources.

Hence, the correct option is (A).

65. The IMF's Board of Governors conducts general quota reviews at regular intervals (no more than five years). Any changes in quotas must be approved by an 85 percent majority of the total voting power, and a member's own quota cannot be changed without its consent.

Hence, the correct option is (B).

66. IDA lends money on concessional terms. This means that IDA credits have a zero or very low-interest charge and repayments are stretched over 30 to 38 years, including a 5 to 10-year grace period. IDA also provides grants to countries at risk of debt distress.

Hence, the correct option is (D).

67. The Organization of the Petroleum Exporting Countries (OPEC) is an intergovernmental organization of twelve oil-producing countries made up of Algeria, Angola, Ecuador, Iran, Iraq, Kuwait, Libya, Nigeria, Qatar, Saudi Arabia, the United Arab Emirates, and Venezuela.

Hence, the correct option is (B).

68. The subsidy contains three basic elements are a financial contribution, by a government or any public body within the region of an element, which confers an advantage. All three of these elements must be satisfied in order for a subsidy to exist. non-actionable subsidies, however, are not subject to these tariffs.

For example, environmental and scientific subsidies are non-actionable. non-actionable subsidies are those which are functional to explore and pre-competitive development performance, and others that help the disadvantaged region.

Hence, the correct option is (C).

69. A cash book that is used to record the small payments of cash is generally referred to as a petty cash book. The Petty cash book can be expressed as a formal summarization of the petty cash expenditures which refers to the day-to-day normal expenditures of the business which is not related to the direct line of the business.

Hence, the correct option is (D).

70. i) Repayment capacity of loans: reflected by DEBT service coverage ratio.

ii) Profitability performance of the firm reflected by net profit or gross profit ratio or ROI or ROI ratio.

iii) Liquidity position of the firm reflected by current ratio.

Hence, the correct option is (C).

71. The importance of market segmentation is that it allows a business to precisely reach a consumer with specific needs and wants. In the long run, this benefits the company because they are able to use their corporate resources more effectively and make better strategic marketing decisions.

Hence, the correct option is (D).

72. The marketing process consists of elements: strategic marketing analysis, Product, marketing-mix planning, marketing implementation, Demand Flow, Human Needs, and marketing control.

Hence, the correct option is (D).

73. The incorporation of a company is an artificial entity recognized by the law as a legal person that exists independently with rights and liability. This means that a company is treated as a separate person from its participants. It is owned by at least one shareholder and managed by at least one director.

Hence, the correct option is (B).

74. Motivation research is still regarded as an important technique by marketers who want to gain a deeper understanding of why consumers act in the ways that they do. These insights are often thought to be much more revealing than the information provided by traditional descriptive and quantitative marketing research methods Although the term motivation research is most often used to refer to qualitative research that is designed specifically to discover consumers' hidden, tacit, latent, or unconscious motivations.

Hence, the correct option is (A).

75. "A Fundamental Premise of Economics has been that financial incentives are the primary driver of human behavior." The economists then proceed to a consequence of this premise; a focus on a narrow range of "incentive-compatible policies".

Hence, the correct option is (C).

76. The human relations approach is also known as the new Classical approach. Elton Mayo termed it the clinical approach. It attempts to explain the informal relations among employers and employees are concerned with moral and psychological rather than legal aspects of an organization.

Hence, the correct option is (C).

77. In perfect competition, in the long run, there will be no supernormal profit is all the excess profit a firm makes above the minimum return necessary to keep a firm in business.

Supernormal profit is calculated by,

Supernormal profit = Total Revenue – Total Costs

Where total cost includes all fixed and variable costs, plus minimum income necessary for the owner to be happy in that business.

Hence, the correct option is (B).

78. Noncurrent liabilities include debentures, long-term loans, bonds payable, deferred tax liabilities, long-term lease obligations, and pension benefit obligations. The portion of a bond liability that will not be paid within the upcoming year is classified as a noncurrent liability.

Hence, the correct option is (D).

79. The Kyoto Protocol mandated that industrialized nations cut their greenhouse gas emissions at a time when the threat of global warming was growing rapidly. The Protocol was linked to the United Nations Framework Convention on Climate Change (UNFCCC).

Hence, the correct option is (C).

80. Commercial Banks can be further classified into public sector banks, private sector banks, foreign banks, and Regional Rural Banks (RRB). On the other hand, cooperative banks are classified into urban and rural.

Hence, the correct option is (D).

81. Purchase of office equipment for cash will be recorded on the payments side of a cash book. All transactions in the cash book have two sides: debit and credit. All cash receipts are recorded on the left-hand side, and all cash payments are recorded by date on the right-hand side.
Hence, the correct option is (B).

82. Postdated cheques are considered as Accounts receivable. If the postdated check was received as payment on accounts receivable, the accounts receivable balance is not reduced until the date of the check.
Hence, the correct option is (C).

83. Postage stamps on hand are considered as prepaid expenses. Prepaids are any expense the business pays for in advance, such as rent, insurance, office supplies, postage, travel expense, or advances to employees.
Hence, the correct option is (B).

84. Petty cash fund is supposed to be replenished at the end of every accounting period. Replenish means to return the amount of actual cash in the petty cash box back to the amount appearing in the general ledger account Petty Cash. This is done whenever the amount of actual cash in the petty cash box is low and at the end of each accounting period.

Hence, the correct option is (D).

85. A credit balance in the cash book indicates a bank overdraft. Overdrafts are where the bank account becomes negative and the businesses in effect have borrowed from the bank. This is shown in the cash book as a credit balance.

Hence, the correct option is (C).

86. Consistency with reference to application of accounting principles refer to the Accounting methods and procedures used have to be consistently applied from year to year.

Consistency refers to a company's use of accounting principles over time. When accounting principles allow a choice between multiple methods, a company should apply the same accounting method over time.

Hence, the correct option is (C).

87. The journal is the book of chronological record the ledger is the book for the analytical record. The journal, as a book of source entry, ordinarily has greater weight as legal evidence than the ledger.

Hence, the correct option is (B).

88. Unpresented cheques are also referred to as Outstanding cheques. An unpresented check is a check written by a company and entered in its records, but the check has not yet cleared the company's checking account. In other words, the check has not yet been paid by the bank on which the check is drawn. An unpresented check is also known as an outstanding check.

Hence, the correct option is (C).

89. Accrued expenses are considered as a liability. Accrued expenses are typically periodic, and are documented on a company's balance sheet as current liabilities.

Hence, the correct option is (B).

90. Prepaid expenses are considered as Asset. Prepaid expenses are future expenses that have been paid in advance. The number of prepaid expenses that have not yet expired is reported on a company's balance sheet as an asset.

Hence, the correct option is (A).

91. Earned but not yet received income is treated as an asset. It is income earned during a particular accounting period but not received until the end of that period. It is treated as an asset for the business.

Hence, the correct option is (B).

92. Revenue earned but not yet received by the business is known as Accrued revenue. Accrued income is very important in accounting because companies receive advances for their goods or services all the time. To prevent overstating certain accounts, companies need to differentiate between the revenue that they have earned versus revenue that they have not earned yet.

Hence, the correct option is (C).

93. A cash book with a cash bank and discount column is commonly referred to as The prudence concept. Under the prudence concept, do not overestimate the number of revenues recognized or underestimate the number of expenses.

Hence, the correct option is (C).

94. Ownership in business entities can be a sole proprietorship, partnership, or corporation. From the accounting perspective and its purpose, these types of businesses are considered separate entities from their owners. The corporation is only one considered as a separate legal entity.

Hence, the correct option is (D).

95. Prudence is the application of caution in the exercise of the judgments needed in making the estimates required under conditions of uncertainty, such that assets or income are not overstated and liabilities or expenses are not understated. However, the exercise of prudence does not allow, for example, the creation of hidden reserves or excessive provisions, the deliberate understatement of assets or income, or the deliberate overstatement of liabilities or expenses, because the financial statements would not be neutral and therefore, not have the quality or reliability.

Hence, the correct option is (B).

96. The revenue recognition principle dictates that all types of incomes should be recorded or recognized when they are earned. The revenue recognition principle, a combination of accrual accounting and the matching principle, stipulates that revenues are recognized when realized and earned, not necessarily when received.

Hence, the correct option is (C).

97. The matching concept matches revenues with expenses. The matching concept is an accounting practice whereby firms recognize revenues and their related expenses in the same accounting period.

Hence, the correct option is (C).

98. The allocation of the owner's private expenses to his/her business violates the Separate business entity concept. The business entity concept states that the transactions associated with a business must be separately recorded from those of its owners or other businesses.

Hence, the correct option is (C).

99. The accounting period is the time span into which the total life of a business is divided for the purpose of preparing financial statements. This period defines the time range over which business transactions are accumulated into financial statements, and is needed by investors so that they can compare the results of successive time periods.

Hence, the correct option is (C).

100. General Journal, sometimes also known as the book of original entry, because it is the first place a transaction is entered into the books. Journal Entries are made from source documents, which can be anything from receipts to invoices to bank statements.

Hence, the correct option is (B).

101. This kind of delivery involves the delivery of a thing in token of a transfer of some other thing. For example, the key of the godowns with the goods in it, when handed over to the buyer will constitute a symbolic delivery.

Hence, the correct option is (A).

102. If nothing is written about the accounting assumption to be followed it is presumed that they have not been followed. If nothing is written in the financial statements about the fundamental accounting assumptions, then it could be presumed that they have not been followed.

Hence, the correct option is (B).

103. The capital account is a personal account, i.e. an account of a person who is alive. Hence, it can be classified as a personal account. Capital account representing the owner of the business, a person or organisation. Bank account representing the bank, an organization.

Hence, the correct option is (A).

104. A cash account is a Real account as it relates to the property of the business. An account is a list of business transactions falling under the same description for a given period of time. A systematic and summarized record of business transactions with respect to person, property, loss, gain, income, the expense is known as account. An account is generally prepared for one complete year. All accounts other than personal accounts are known as impersonal accounts. For instance, Cash account, Rent account, Wages account, Furniture account are impersonal accounts. Impersonal accounts are classified as Real accounts and Nominal accounts. An account or property or anything owned and possessed by a business is called a real account. In other words, the real account is that account related to assets, objects, etc. of the business. This account consists of assets, and properties that can be seen, touched, measured, purchased and sold. A cash account is a Real account as it relates to the property of the business.

Hence, the correct option is (B).

105. When a payment is made to somebody, you debit the receiver of that payment and credit cash or bank as money is paid from a cash or by means of cheque. When money or cheques are received, you credit the person who is paying you and you debit the cash or bank.

Hence, the correct option is (A).

106. The cost concept requires that all assets are recorded in the book of accounts at their purchase price, which includes the cost of acquisition, transportation, installation and making the asset ready to use. For example, an old plant was purchased for Rs. 50 lakh, which is into the business of manufacturing detergent powder. The following were the other expenses incurred for its installation:
1. Transporting the plant to the factory site- Rs. 10,000
2. Repairs for bringing the plant into running position-Rs.15,000
3. Installation-Rs.25,000
The total amount at which the plant will be recorded in the books of account would be the sum of all these, i.e. Rs. 50,50,000.
The concept of cost is historical in nature as it is something, which has been paid on the date of acquisition and does not change year after year. This cost is also called as original cost or historical cost.
Hence, the correct option is (D).

107. Sales – Gross Profit = Cost of goods sold
Gross profit is the profit a company makes after deducting the costs associated with making and selling its products, or the costs associated with providing its services. Gross profit will appear on a company's income statement and can be calculated by subtracting the cost of goods sold (COGS) from revenue (sales).

Hence, the correct option is (A).

108. There are mainly three types of accounts: Real, Personal and Nominal accounts. All assets of a firm, which are tangible or intangible, fall under the category "Real accounts". Tangible real accounts are related to those things that can be touched and physically felt. Few examples of tangible real accounts are buildings, machinery, stock, land, etc. Intangible real accounts are those which can't be touched and physically felt. Few examples of intangible real accounts are trademarks, patents, goodwill, etc.

Hence, the correct option is (A).

109. Valuation of stock in accounting follows the principle of cost price or Net realizable Value whichever is lower.
It is valued at Cost price or Realisable Value, whichever is less. It is based on the principle of Conservatism or prudence, According to which all anticipated losses should be recorded in the books of accounts, but all anticipated or unrealized gains should be ignored.

Hence, the correct option is (C).

110. Nominal accounts in accounting are the temporary accounts, such as the income statement accounts. In other words, nominal accounts are the accounts that report revenues, expenses, gains, and losses. In the above question, all the

accounts are revenue/expense accounts except for Outstanding Salaries account which is a liability account, the balance of which will appear on the balance sheet.

Hence, the correct option is (A).

111. A fixed asset is an asset of a business held with the intention of being used for the purpose of producing or providing goods or services and is not held for sale in the normal course of business.

They can be categorized as:

Vehicle: This will include the car you use for business purposes provided it is registered in the business's name or the name of the founder.

Furniture & Fixtures: This will include the desks, chairs, workstations and the other fittings in your office work station.

Computer Equipment: As the name suggests, this will include the desktops, laptops, routers, dongles and data-storage devices used for business purposes.

Office Equipment: This will include the air-conditioner, water-dispenser, microwave, telephone, refrigerator, etc. that are used in your office or business premises

Hence, the correct option is (C).

112. A trader calculated his profit as Rs.150000 on 31/03/2014. It is an event.
Financial accounting is the process of recording, summarizing and reporting a company's business transactions through financial statements. These statements are the income statement, the balance sheet, the cash flow statement and the statement of retained earnings.
Hence, the correct option is (B).

113. The principle of double-entry system of accounting is "Every debit has a corresponding credit" hence the total of all debits has to be equal to the total of all credits. In simple words, every business transaction affects two accounts. If one account is debited the other account will be credited with a similar amount.

For example, if the business purchases machinery worth Rs. 5,00,000, then machinery account gets debited with amount Rs. 5,00,000 as the business is receiving an asset for its operation, on the other side cash account automatically gets credited with the same amount of Rs. 5,00,000 as cash is going out of business.

Hence, the correct option is (D).

114. Historical cost is the original cost of an asset, as recorded in an entity's accounting records. Many of the transactions recorded in an organization's accounting records are stated at their historical cost. This concept is clarified by the cost principle, which states that you should only record an asset, liability, or equity investment at its original acquisition cost.

Hence, the correct option is (A).

115. The comparison of the financial statement of one year with that of another is possible only when the consistency concept is followed. The accounting information provided by the financial statements would be useful in drawing conclusions regarding the working of an enterprise only when it allows comparisons over a

period of time as well as with the working of other enterprises. Thus, both inter-firm and inter-period comparisons are required to be made. This can be possible only when accounting policies and practices followed by enterprises are uniform and are consistent over the period of time.

Hence, the correct option is (C).

116. Profit and loss are calculated at the stage of summarising.

Calculating Profit is a common way of 'calculating the total expenses' and total Profit earned by any business during a particular time. The detailed Report on Profit and loss help in making future decisions on how to cut down the Expenses and Increase Profit of the Business. It all involves the collection of data, summarising it and finally, it is calculated at the stage known as Classifying.

Hence, the correct option is (D).

117. They depict not only profits and losses, but even assets and liabilities solving tax disputes with tax authorities. Let's take a look at the objectives of financial statements along with their features. They even help readers of these statements know the accounting policies used in them. These statements also provide information relating to the company's cash flows.

Hence, the correct option is (D).

118. Statutory operation is public enterprises brought into existence by a special Act of the Parliament. A holding company is a company that owns other companies" outstanding stock. A subsidiary company is a company that is which is called the parent e company.

Hence, the correct option is (D).

119. Accounts relating to income, revenue, gain, expenses and losses are termed as nominal accounts. These accounts are also known as fictitious accounts as they do not represent any tangible asset. A separate account is maintained for each head or expense or loss and gain or income. Wages account, Rent account, Commission account, Interest received accounts are some examples of nominal account.

The rule for nominal accounts is Debit all expenses and losses Credit all incomes and gains.

Hence, the correct option is (C).

120. An important concept of accrual accounting, the matching principle states that the related revenues and expenses must be matched in the same period. This is done in order to link the costs of an asset or revenue to its benefits.

Hence, the correct option is (D).

// Notes //

period of time as well as with the working of other enterprises. Thus, both inter-firm and inter-period comparisons are required to be made. This can be possible only when accounting policies and practices followed by enterprises are uniform and are consistent over the period of time.

Hence, the correct option is (C).

116. Profit and loss are calculated at the stage of summarising.

Calculating Profit is a common way of 'calculating the total expenses' and total Profit earned by any business during a particular time. The detailed Report on Profit and loss help in making future decisions on how to cut down the Expenses and Increase Profit of the Business. It all involves the collection of data, summarising it and finally, it is calculated at the stage known as Classifying.

Hence, the correct option is (D).

117. They depict not only profits and losses, but even assets and liabilities solving tax disputes with tax authorities. Let's take a look at the objectives of financial statements along with their features. They even help readers of these statements know the accounting policies used in them. These statements also provide information relating to the company's cash flows.

Hence, the correct option is (D).

118. Statutory operation is public enterprises brought into existence by a special Act of the Parliament. A holding company is a company that owns other companies" outstanding stock. A subsidiary company is a company that is which is called the parent e company.

Hence, the correct option is (D).

119. Accounts relating to income, revenue, gain, expenses and losses are termed as nominal accounts. These accounts are also known as fictitious accounts as they do not represent any tangible asset. A separate account is maintained for each head or expense or loss and gain or income. Wages account, Rent account, Commission account, Interest received accounts are some examples of nominal account.

The rule for nominal accounts is Debit all expenses and losses Credit all incomes and gains.

Hence, the correct option is (C).

120. An important concept of accrual accounting, the matching principle states that the related revenues and expenses must be matched in the same period. This is done in order to link the costs of an asset or revenue to its benefits.

Hence, the correct option is (D).

// Notes //

// Notes //